DR. JAN KOPIA

PLAYING VIDEO GAMES TO LEARN

A parents' guide to educational gaming for kids

*Includes **50 pages** of existing **game suggestions!***

Dedicated to my children Desmond, Darrion, and Fionella, who spent so much time playing all kinds of games with me. You have shown me a practical side beyond the endless hours of researching literature and interviews. It is wonderful to see you growing!

PLAYING VIDEO GAMES TO LEARN

JAN KOPIA

CONTENTS

About the Author

I. Part One: 6

1. Introduction....................7
2. Weighing In Modern Gadgets....................12
3. Internet 31
4. Status Of Scientific Research 44

II. Part Two: 48

5. Why You Should Encourage Gaming 49
6. Your Role In Your Child's Game-Based Learning 55
7. Evaluating Your Child's Gaming Content 73
8. The Parent's Guide To The Educational Gaming World 77
9. Educational Games for Preschoolers (4-7) 94
10. Educational Gaming Platforms for Young Kids (5-9 years) 106
11. Educational Gaming Platforms for Tweens (9-12 years) 119
12. Educational Gaming Platforms for Teenagers (12 and up) 134
13. The Little Hacker: Learning Programming Skills For The Future.139
14. The Power Of Motivation: Gamification Strategies 144
15. Tying The Knot: Getting It All Together Conclusions 149

References

ABOUT THE AUTHOR_

Dr. Jan Kopia has worked with kids for almost 15 years. He began his career teaching highly talented children advanced topics with a focus on science and technology.

He is involved in research and technological development in the educational field and beyond, besides raising his children and working in the IT business.

PART ONE:_

THE BIG DIGITAL PICTURE

INTRODUCTION_

PARENTING HAS BECOME one of the most neglected aspects of human life. It's a trend that became palpable at the beginning of the twenty-first century, and its subsequent effects have never been as devastating. There are many reasons why the contagious disease of bad parenting has eaten deep into the flesh of society, but one of the largest causes is unpreparedness. It cannot be denied that many parents and teachers have made no attempt to acquire the skills and knowledge necessary for parenting and teaching using the tools and method offered by modern technologies. The result is often an ill-parented child regarding the useful handling of modern gadgets of information technology.

Parenting is the process of promoting and maintaining the overall growth of a child from infancy to adulthood. *Good* parenting – especially regarding the use of technological tools and toys- involves employing effective measures in the upbringing of a child that result in a noticeable improvement in their physical, emotional, social and intellectual development. *Bad* parenting involves purposeful, or unintentional, utilization of a series of measures in a child's upbringing that can gravely harm their all-round development.

Knowing and implementing the right measures to raise a child is no superficial task. It requires a lot of hard work, foresight, and sacrifice. Psychologists and researchers alike have observed and recorded the results: the failure to put in the much needed work in a child's upbringing can form mild psychological disorders. For example, the child may develop the inability to make or keep friends and healthy relationships, or suffer from depression and low self-esteem. The availability of new technologies enhances this effect by offering easy distractions. On the other hand, new technologies also offer opportunities to take the right measures.

A good parent understands themselves *and* their children, then uses that knowledge to create an effective regimen of activities that builds their children in character, intellect, and compassion – not by denying but especially by using modern technologies. But how can you acquire this knowledge? This book answers these (and many more) questions by providing education and recommendations that are handy in real life situations regarding the use of video games and gaming equipment with the focus on game-based learning

Welcome to the 21st Century

The 21st century is witnessing a revolutionary expansion of the technology bubble creating new technological ideas on a regular basis. Routine tasks, such as sending and receiving postal letters to keep in touch with loved ones have become incredibly easier with our use of exceedingly complex – yet simply crafted – gadgets including smartphones, tablets and laptop devices. However, while these technological advancements have been welcomed , they have brought with them negatives, especially in the way they have affected the attitudes of children but also of parents. Studies[1-5] have shown that a staggering number of kids possess or have access to smartphones, and most of them are perpetually connected to social media platforms. It follows logic to assume that time spent on these devices is time not spent involved in other activities, such as reading and physical exercise.

Technology has had massive effects in the way children interact with their immediate environment and with other people around them in contrast to children of earlier generations. Although social media can be used for educational purposes, its overuse has been found to have a negative effect on children's self-esteem and self-confidence, and their all-round personal development [6].

> In earlier days, kids were punished with house arrest. Due to their massive in-house engagements with technology, kids are now punished by asking them to go outside.

One of the most pronounced differences in the way children live today in industrial countries, as opposed to previous generations, is that they don't get as much exercise. This is due mostly to the fact that technology (such as tablets, smartphones and gaming consoles) encourages them to be sedentary when they get home from school. And why would they when they have all the entertainment they need in the palm of their hands? As a result, fewer and fewer children go outside and play with other kids, and we've seen childhood obesity rates rise drastically over the past several decades. In 2012, the rate was 18%, which is 11% higher than it was in 1980[7]. The same study also states that more than 33% of all kids and youth were overweight or obese. While many schools and parents have put in measures to curb this trend by promoting organized exercise both during and after school, we still have a long way to go in helping children assume a more active lifestyle.

Another effect that technology has had on children is in the way they interact with other children. Children who spend more time on their devices have minimal time left to spend with their peers, and tend to find it more difficult to pick up on social cues and develop meaningful relationships. This can develop into a serious emotional problem as they grow and develop.

The aim of this book is not to rule out the many uses of technology altogether, but rather to serve as a guide to parents who want the best for their children by using technology the right way. Technology offers endless possibilities of positive usage in a child's learning, and can prove indispensable in their upbringing if utilized correctly.

The 21st Century Parent

Every parent wants what's best for their children. And to achieve this, they often implement strategies that help shape their children into successful adults while avoiding those that may result in maladaptive outcomes. As a parent in this digital age, you must understand that absolute control over your child's development cannot be achieved or pursued nor is it useful. Instead, an approach of mutual understanding, between parent and child, must be employed to tackle the many setbacks to good parenting in this modern era. A way of achieving this mutual understanding is by recognizing your child's needs at various stages of their growth and development and adjusting your attitude to suit their needs.

It's safe to conclude that the parenting burdens on a 21st century parent supersede those that earlier generations parents bore. This conclusion is drawn from the facts and figures surrounding the behaviors and attitudes of contemporary children, due partly to the direct effects of modern society, economy, the advancements in the technology of the era and partly to the ever-increasing levels of 'urbanization' and 'civilization' brought about by same technological advancements. The environment is always changing, and as such, children's attitudes are evolving; a result of which is an ever present need for parents to adjust their behavioral and parental patterns. Somewhat in the 20th century, for instance, a parent may have faced a challenge of keeping their children indoors more, to prevent them from coming to harm in the process of playing with other children. In this era, in contrast, a parent would be worried about the time their children spend indoors glued to their smartphones or televisions.

Innovations in technology have made the arduous task of parenting even more labor demanding. More than ever, children spending too much time on digital technology is considered injurious to their mental, physical, emotional and intellectual health. Children and adults are becoming increasingly timid and short of confidence due to over-indulgence in social media. All of these negative effects are happening in an era when parents are saddled with the responsibility of combining child upbringing *and* day-to-day-work.

The roles and responsibilities of parents towards their children in the modern era are more complex, and there's no quick fix for the uphill task. However, there are certain guidelines and recommendations that, if adhered to, may bring about positive outcomes in the upbringing of your kids. "Parents are not born, they are made." The role of this book is to outline the unique challenges modern era parents face in the course of parenting throughout digital gaming content, and present guidelines and recommendations to help surmount them.

TECHNOLOGICAL GADGETS HAVE BECOME a mainstay in our lives. How could you leave the house a few years ago without a mobile phone, or not be available all day or arrange to meet someone on the road? How did one get answers to important questions or the news of the world and how did one stay in contact with distant people? From mobile phones to desktop computers, heart rate monitors to blood glucose sensors, intelligent watches and rings, electronic devices have become an extra appendage in our anatomy. Although children and adults share certain devices in common – including mobile phones and computers – some of these machines are age sensitive and used almost exclusively by specific age groups. Health monitors for blood glucose and heart rate sensors are only generally used by older people, while younger people favor more trivial gadgets such as gaming consoles and digital toys. As a parent, it's important to know what gadgets are suitable for your children and how they impact them.

Personal Computers

Personal computers (PCs), like most devices, have undergone tremendous evolutions in the last few decades. Homes – and even offices – are shifting from bulky desktop computers to the more portable and sleek notebooks and laptops. Notebooks and laptops are favored by children, as opposed to desktops, because of their relatively small sizes and ease of handling. This is not to say that desktop computers have outlived their importance, in fact, they are still held in large numbers by many homes, primarily for their lower costs, better performance and longevity.

Computers can be powerful tools for child education. They have the ability to run thousands software programs, and offer quick access to the internet and other sources of data, which can enhance intra- and extracurricular learning experiences. There is also a myriad of educative games that can be run on a computer. These include tactical board games, strategy games, action games, word games and learning and critical thinking games; all of these have a potential to improve the quality of education a child gets. Aside from learning and playing on then computer, you could also teach your child how to type quickly. Good typing is an important but sadly often neglected skill that can be learned at home. There are tons of paid and free computer programs available for learning and teaching typing in software stores that you can use to get your child grounded in this indispensable skill. As technology grows, it will only become *more* important that a child needs to learn how to type. On the other hand, voice input and alternative input forms are evolving as well, so typing may soon no longer be necessary.

While computers can be put to effective use to educate children, overuse can make them just as harmful as they are beneficial. Care must be taken to ensure that children are spending the right amount of time with their PCs.

PC's come in different designs. Desktop computers are typically structured to have an external display screen and an external keyboard, which are plugged into USB ports on the back of the tower. Desktop computers are popular for home and business computing applications as they leave space on the desk for multiple monitors. Laptops, on the other hand, are designed to be portable. Usually, all of the laptop's hardware required to operate it, such as the motherboard, display screen, power ports, processors, are built into a single unit. Laptops are increasingly preferred to desktops because of their portability and ease of handling. However, a major advantage that desktops have over laptops is that they are usually more upgradable and cost-effective than laptops. Since the components of laptop devices are tightly built into a single unit, it is not manufacturer recommended (and sometimes not even possible) to improve the overall design of the computer or add extra internal components.

Another type of PC's to consider is the netbook. Netbooks are smaller, lighter and cheaper versions of notebook computers, and are sometimes referred to as mini notebooks or mini laptops. They are designed to be even smaller and more compact, and can carry out only basic computing tasks and access the internet. Since their inception in 2007, netbook computers have undergone hardware evolutions overtime, so much that the only consequential distinctions between a modern netbook and its notebook counterpart lie simply in their relative sizes and prices. The device types are merging more and more.

Gaming computers are another variant of personal computers. They are essentially standard computers built to provide a high-end gaming experience through high performance hardware such as powerful video cards and processors in order to handle the requirements of demanding 3d video games. Gaming computers can be laptops or desktop computers.

The choice of the type of computer to get for your child depends solely on you. Irrespective of brand and model, most personal computers perform similar basic tasks such as typing, internet usage, running educational and simple gaming programs, to nearly the same degree. The only difference is the 3D-performance which is not required in learning games because the lag of offers of educational games which use modern 3D-technologies. The only major differentiating factor between these computers is the platform on which their programs are run. These platforms are called operating systems (OS). The four commonly used operating systems in the world of computers today are Windows, Mac OS, Linux, and Chrome OS.

Figure 3.1: PCs can be used for educational gaming, among other uses.

The Windows operating system is developed by Microsoft and can be run in most personal computers, towers and laptops alike. The latest edition, as at the time of this writing, of Windows is Windows 10.1. The Mac OS, unlike Windows, is an operating system that only runs on Apple computers. Linux is an open-source operating system software that is based on the Linux kernel. Chrome OS is another type of operating system, developed by Google and based on the Linux kernel. It is designed primarily to support web applications. For games in general, but also in the area of educational games, Windows is more suitable, as there is a larger selection of educational games.

> Computers have suffered plummeting market shares since the emergence and explosion of smartphones. PC makers recorded a decrease by 48% in year-on-year profits in 2012 [8]

High-end computers are more expensive and more powerful and offer a range of services that is not obtainable by their low-cost counterparts. Notwithstanding, most educational games can well be run on 'normal' PCs, and do *not* require the high-end graphics capabilities that high-end computers offer. The following points are intended to help you choose the right computer:

- How big is your budget for a computer?

A gaming laptop quickly costs a few thousand, a netbook or chromebook just a few hundred. Simple learning games or Internet use is already possible with the inexpensive devices.

- Are only educational games important or would I like to make modern 3D games possible for the child?

Since there are - unfortunately - hardly any modern 3D learning games, the only question here is whether the child would like (or is allowed) to play other games as well.

- Does the device have to be carried around?

This question goes in the direction of laptop or desktop (Learning-) games run equally on all of them.

- Which selection is important to me?

The selection of educational games is larger for Windows than for MacOS or Linux. If you're an Apple user, you might tend towards MacOS for your child.

Smartphones and Tablets

Before the emergence of smartphones, computers (desktops and notebooks) offered pretty much the only solution to electronic learning. The handhelds from earlier times, which were mostly equipped with LCD displays and very basic 2d games, did not offer any significant learning experience. Though there were smartphones before Apple's iPhone, it was this invention that triggered a hype that has been unstoppable ever since.

Figure 3.2: Kids playing on their smartphones – the smartphone is by far the most common gaming platform for children.

Since 2007, people have been using the smartphone so intensively that it has replaced the PC more and more in terms of market share for information research, games, general Internet use, and communication. Additionally, the 2010 introduction of the iPad, a tablet-style computer with a larger portable display another technical revolution. In addition to Apple, many other manufacturers brought smartphones and tablets to the market and revolutionized the use of electronic devices fundamentally.

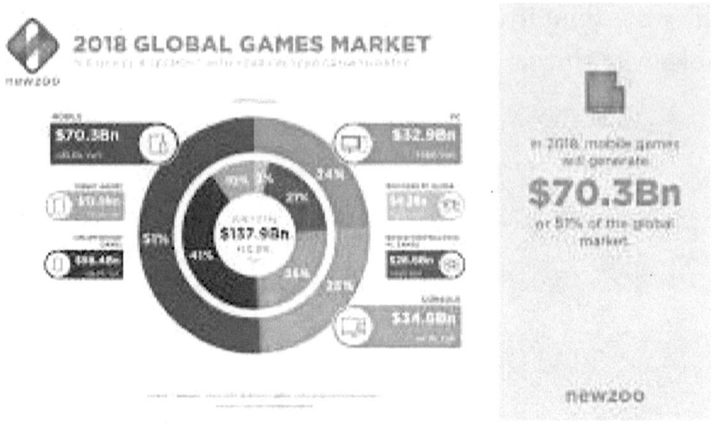

Figure 3.3: Market share analysis of the 2018 global games market

Smartphones and tablet devices have made it possible to use mobile applications, or apps, for short. Apps are nothing more than programs that can be installed, just like computer programs can be installed on computers. The main difference between computer programs and mobile apps lies in their relative complexity and price. With over 2 million apps (in 2018) in each of the leading online stores ("App Store" from Apple and "Play Store" from Google), the options for mobile apps are nearly endless. As children are increasingly using smartphones, tablets and other handheld devices, the age appropriateness of mobile apps becomes an important factor to consider. Unfortunately, there are hardly any age-based standards or orientation aids that are applied worldwide to develop programs and applications suitable for children. In this context, developers of mobile apps have the liberty to design and release apps as they deem fit, without recourse to age appropriateness of the apps. Even when end users complain about inappropriateness in applications the apps are simply deleted from the stores in most cases, leaving the issue of the implementation of much needed standards unattended (See chapter 7).

Figure 3.4: Forecast for the 2012-2021 global games market

Currently, there are few differences between tablets and smartphones in regards to the kind of apps they can run. Most apps work on a wide variety of devices and to the same degree. However, due to their differing screen sizes and technological specifications, the same app can look and work differently on smartphones than on tablets. Tablets offer the advantage of a much larger screen (but usually with resolutions similar to those of smartphones) and compatibility with other interactive devices (such as pens which can be used for educational purposes very well). Despite these seemingly impressive advantages of tablets over smartphones, tablet sales are declining the world over; this has led to developers offering mobile apps in only smartphone-optimized versions. Nevertheless, there are mobile apps that offer outstanding operation with great user comfort, especially on tablet devices, and have great potential to serve as examples of positive developments in human-machine interaction for future devices.

Smartphones and tablets have been available for less than 10 years. Therefore, studies and scientific research in this field are currently scarce and hardly consequential due to the lack of long-term studies. However, there are varying opinions on what the dangers of tablet and smartphone use are for society at large, and specifically for children. The hazards posed by the use of these devices are still under-examined and very few studies have provided any meaningful information about their long-term effects. Consequently, all current discussions in the journalistic, pedagogical, or scientific fields are important, but not generally valid in terms of making inferences and drawing conclusions.

Figure 3.5: Although on a decline in market shares, the tablet remains one of the most popular gaming devices for kids, especially kids between 6 and 12.

Consoles and Handhelds

Gaming hardware described here includes devices that are intended for recreational gaming use. There are a myriad of gaming devices available in the market today, but the most known (and still available) ones are the Sony PlayStation, Nintendo DS, Microsoft Xbox, and Nintendo Switch.

Since the introduction of the earliest gaming devices such as the "Gameboy" (in 1989), the area of gaming has witnessed revolutionary technological innovations, mostly reflected by advancements in graphical performance, however, game concepts and ideas have remained largely the same. Among the innovations worth noting after the invention of the first "handhelds" and stationary consoles are the Wii Controllers with

Motion Detection (2006) - also called Wii Motion Controllers - and the PlayStation VR (2016). The motion detection of the controllers made it possible for players to associate their own body movements with the game (such as throwing a ball, swinging heavily, etc.), something that had previously only been possible through a game controller. Nintendo developed the Wii nunchuk controllers as an innovative technology; using the body movement provided by these controllers is important to children, and during the learning experience in general – using the Wii nunchuk together with a learning game can enhance the learning experience. The Wii nunchuk controllers are a very good input device for game-based learning, which no other manufacturer reproduced in such a successful manner (Microsoft Kinect technology was not successful in the market and PlayStation move is a niche product with a recent improved development for Sony's VR gaming). Recent products such as the Nintendo Switch, however, go a step backwards in regards to body and controller movement, even though motion detection is built in almost every controller nowadays. Nevertheless, it is still possible to make punches and move swords with these controllers just by moving the arms and body.

Figure 3.6: Nintendo 2DS XL

While all of this was going on, gaming companies were in intensive competition with PC games manufacturers. In fact, reports in 2018 showed that the market share of traditional gaming hardware manufacturers and PC games developers stood at roughly same values – with PC games producers having a slight advantage. However, this advantage is expected to take a U-turn in coming years, as console games are forecasted to overtake PC games in the year 2020 (figure 3.4). In comparison with the smartphone market potential, the battle is already lost.

Despite this development, the choices in the field of game-based learning for consoles are very limited, especially for the most recent consoles. In fact, most learning games exist for Nintendo consoles, specifically the Wii and the Nintendo DS – both older devices. As parents, it might be useful to purchase a used Wii or Wii U with existing Wii games to enjoy a wise selection of games with learning experiences for kids (see chapter 8).

Today, games are published on multiple devices and can be played in the same manner, and to similar levels of complexity and quality on PC,

PlayStation, Xbox and Nintendo devices, making it increasingly difficult to choose between the platforms. Nevertheless, there still are marked differences in the available game genres across platforms. The following is an overview of the general features and functionalities of the various gaming platforms.

Nintendo

Nintendo's target group is the younger generation. This applies in particular to the handheld products of the Nintendo DS series. Nintendo itself develops various game series that have enjoyed great popularity for years. These are usually also the most popular games for the consoles, although other game developers also publish great titles for Nintendo consoles. Nintendo developed some of the most well known game series such as Super Mario, Legend of Zelda, and Pokémon. Nintendo games are specifically made for and targeted to children in early ages; though there are few games for the Nintendo DS or Nintendo Switch that are not suitable for children under 12 years (or even higher ages), the bulk of Nintendo games are child-friendly and suitable for a wide range of ages.

Figure 3.7: Nintendo Switch

Nintendo DS and the consoles developed on it are intended for children of young age (from the age of 6 years). The WiiU, Switch, etc., and some contents are also designed for children 6 years or older. Furthermore, the handling of the consoles – menu guidance when changing games, saving, updating software etc. – is made particularly for young children (especially the DS series of consoles). Most educational games on the console market for kids exist for the Nintendo DS or the Wii(U). Parental control is also available.

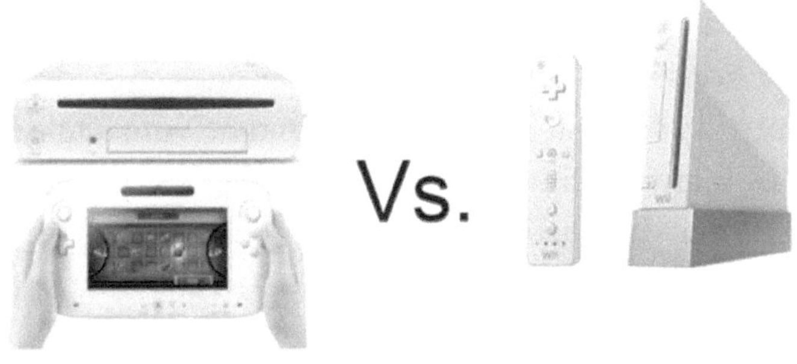

Figure 3.8: Nintendo Wii U and Nintendo Wii

PlayStation and Xbox

The gaming consoles by Sony and Microsoft thrive on blockbuster games. Both console providers focus on a broad age spectrum among the target group. Therefore, there is no special focus of the style of games, neither in genre nor in presentation. This can also be seen in the selection, which was usually considerably higher for the PlayStation console generations than for Nintendo's gaming devices or the Xbox. The selection ranges from cute cartoon platformers to brutal shooters. Both PlayStation and Xbox are suitable for players aged 12-14 or older. This general statement is based on the generally available games for these consoles. However, there are individual games that are suitable for younger children.

The Microsoft Xbox 360 and Sony PS3, though are both older version gaming platforms, offer a wider variety of games your child would enjoy playing even though the choice for educational games is limited. As an added advantage, because they are relatively old devices (as the Nintendo Wii) in the gaming sphere, you can find cheap, discounted models that your child can practice on before you invest in more expensive alternatives. If you have children in different age groups, the

Xbox 360 or PS3 may be better choices than newer, more advanced machines such as the Xbox One or PS4, as it'll give your younger kids some good options while keeping your older ones entertained. You'd still however, need to regulate the gaming content your children would be exposed to, as there are titles such as Grant Theft Auto and Call of Duty, whose content may be unsuited to younger children. These games can be replaced sports games or cool adventure or arcade games that offer less mature content.

Figure 3.9: Sony PlayStation 3

If your child is highly passionate about games, then you might consider the pricier, newer consoles, like the Microsoft Xbox One S, Xbox One X, Sony PlayStation 4 and PlayStation 4 Pro. Sony has the edge for serious gaming families with its PlayStation VR headset designed to work with the PS4 and PS4 Pro. PlayStation VR headsets provide an intensely immersive, virtual reality game experience. Xbox One S is a better choice for families who already own a lot of Xbox games, as it will run some Xbox 360 games.

With our view set on games strictly for learning, the options for Xbox and PlayStation varieties (such as 3, 4 and VR) are limited. Therefore, they may be considered poor choices of console for kids eager to dive into the world of educational gaming. Healthy options of educational games are given in chapter 8.

Unfortunately, the options of gaming consoles is not endless. Since early manufacturers such as *Mega Drive, DreamCast* and *SEGA* have pulled out of the race, *Nintendo, Microsoft* and *Sony* have formed the bedrock the modern gaming world. A much easier way of making your choice, though not always right, is to simply ask your children what they want.

Choosing the right gaming platform for your kids shouldn't be a huge problem. Your choice should for the most part be based on their age and their thirst for gaming. With games such as Super Mario Party, Monster Hunter Generations Ultimate, Octopath Traveler, or Mario Tennis Aces, as well as thrilling activity packs such as the Labo Toy-Con Variety Kit, Nintendo maintains its position as the best option for young children (age between 5-10). Using the nunchuk or other motion controller input devices, kids can use their entire body to play most games. There is also a wide variety of educational games for Nintendo consoles (especially the Wii and DS series), which will be elaborated later in this book. The Nintendo Switch works both as a stationary console that plugs into your TV and a carry-around gaming device with two built-in controllers and a touchscreen..

With the exception of the Nintendo DS and the Wii, learning content is very rare on gaming consoles, which is the reason why consoles other than these are not recommended for learning purposes by this book.

Figure 3.10: Microsoft Xbox 360

Benefits and Dangers of Using Modern Game-based Learning Gadgets

The surge in technological innovations has revolutionized the way people live and interact with one another. Technological advancements have made computers, wireless communication, telemedicine, smartphones, rocket science, self-driving cars and artificial intelligence, which were little beyond farfetched imaginations just decades ago, an invigorating reality. The world of gadgets for game-based learning have become a major part of our children's daily lives, so much so that they can't imagine living without them.

Advantages of Modern Game-based learning Gadgets

The benefits of contemporary game-based learning gadgets are innumerable and vital, and it's a daunting task to even attempt putting all of these benefits into this book. However, the most basic examples of modern gadgets benefits are as follows:

1. Game-based learning is a tested and proven method of imparting essential knowledge and skills in children [11]. Learning by playing is within the nature of human beings. People from an early age and impart knowledge and skills through motivating play.
2. The concept of educational gaming offers another dimension to the world of learning, as it provides kids with a different perspective of learning than the ones they are used to. Take the VR experience for instance, kids who engage with the VR can "be anywhere at any time" due to the virtual possibilities it offers.
3. Kids with disabilities are able to benefit from these technologies as well. Most educational games leave room for participation of large groups, including disabled children.

Some dangers Posed by Modern Game-based learning Gadgets

Although these new generation gadgets offer a seemingly endless stream of benefits and uses, they have also caused excessive amounts of harm that was simply nonexistent before their arrival.

1. They can be addictive.
2. 1. Over-indulgence in the less physically demanding act of gaming can often hinder in a child's participation in a more physically tasking, and usually better, activity such as

swimming, playing basketball and "hide and seek". There are still open questions about the influence of games regarding the cognitive and physical effects, e.g. ADD / ADHD, epilepsy etc.

3. Exaggerated engagement with electronic gaming can also affect the player's cognitive and emotional prowess negatively [6].
4. There are health hazards posed by overexposure to the radiation emitted by these tech gadgets (though there's a shortage of scientific studies in this regard).
5. Privacy and security concerns are another issue to look out for.

The fields of research dealing with the consequences of media use are manifold - psychology, education, other fields of medicine and health, socially and technology. There will therefore always be different perspectives, theories, and advice, depending on the research area in focus. After several decades of discussion, no uniform conclusions of what content should be sensibly allowed for what age groups using what media. Knowing this, parents must take responsibility and decide what they feel is right for their kids.

THE BIRTH of the Internet

The Internet as it is today did not arise from a need for better communication, information or entertainment purposes. Owing to the necessity of coordinating defense resources in the United States, the US Department of Defense Advanced Research Project Agency (ARPA) came up with an ingenious way of dividing information into smaller bits, or packets, and transferred them between computers. This soon led to two other satellite networks, and the idea became widespread in some closed communities, majorly the science and the military. But the Internet as we commonly know it now was not to develop until a British Knight, Sir Tim Berners-Lee, came up with the design of the World Wide Web and the Uniform Resources Locator (URL) in the 1980s which with the identification of resources in the web was possible.

By the early 1990s, the restriction of who could use the Internet had been lifted and commercialization began. Different businesses came online one way or the other, such that at the beginning of the new millennium, more than 1000 American newspapers had come online, offering their contents to users free of charge – Homepages developed everywhere. Today, all media is online - the radio, the television, the media- and publishing industry, and the capability of the Internet has been shown to be limitless. But what really is the Internet?

Figure 4.1: As of June 2018, **55.1%** of the world's population has internet access – Wikipedia

The Internet is a network of networks. Each network on the internet connects computers ranging from two to over a thousand, and the only way each of these networks could be made to communicate with each other and share resources is to have a single network that connects them all. That single network is the Internet. It should be borne in mind that the Internet is not just the World Wide Web. Rather, the Internet is made up of several applications and standards. Emailing, for example, is a separate Internet application, done via the internet. The same applies to downloading and uploading files on the Internet using standard protocols.

Most Internet applications are used via a web browser (Google Chrome, Mozilla Firefox, Microsoft Internet Explorer, Edge, Apple Safari etc.). You really do not need a web browser to be able to use some services over the Internet. The exchange of data, e.g. for emails, chat communication, transmission of data in games, etc., is carried out via other programs which execute the respective devices.

Online games are not a separate type of video game. Any game - no matter on which platform it is played - can be an online game as soon as player data is transferred or other players are also from the party via the Internet. It is a trend of today's games that many games bring with them the requirement of an Internet connection - on the one hand to be able to receive constant updates, on the other hand to be able to use collaborative gaming functions.

The Good, the Bad, and the Ugly

These different mediums in which games can be played online allow the use of multimedia content. Gaming platforms also include chat features that allow players to exchange ideas and socialize. These things make it necessary for a parent to monitor their children's involvement in online games and online collaboration, as online communities can be "the good", "the bad", and "the ugly" on the Internet. In the next section in this chapter, each of these consequences will be discussed in further detail.

- **The Good**

For the purpose of *good* in this section of the chapter, let's just regard it is as what is fair and confers benefits, as opposed to harm. The good in the Internet, in general, is almost innumerable. In online collaboration and gaming specifically, there are equal benefits for participants of all ages and with or without any cognitive or physical disabilities. These benefits will be discussed in the section about the Internet in general.

Education

The Internet in general, and online gaming in particular, offers a great opportunity and potential to learn. Since the Internet became available to the public in the 1990s, its spreading and commercialization has led to improvements in the terms of design as well as use. Therefore, it is not strange to find millions of web resources that can be used for research, teaching and learning. These resources have increased and improved tremendously over the years starting from pure encyclopedia-like resources to all sort of different formats of information. the. One example that makes information on many subject readily available is Wikipedia, a free online encyclopedia contributed to by any interested person. Just about any imaginable subject or topic has a Wikipedia entry. However, its greatest challenge is ensuring the accuracy of the information provided, a challenge that makes Wikipedia less acceptable for academic references but a good starting point for every research.

With different webpages designed for general and specific topics, the opportunity to learn and share knowledge on any of these topics is limitless. This is also true for content of the increasing market share of streamed media. From streamed documentaries, movies, and TV shows, to self-made movies on platforms such as YouTube, the options of the content to select from is overwhelming. The same applies to news feeds from Twitter/Facebook/Instagram etc., weblogs, podcasts, newsletters, RSS feeds and many other formats. Parents need to make careful decisions about the content their kids are consuming since age rating is typically not put in place throughout all offers.

Team Work

One of the many things the Internet has facilitated is teamwork over long distances. In fact, teamwork is the very reason why the Internet and the web were invented in the first place. The need to facilitate cooperation and knowledge and information sharing in the military and scientific communities was why the ARPANET was developed.. The interaction channels have evolved from simple text messaging to video and telephone conferencing - interactive Kanban boards, voice-chats, ticket systems and whiteboard functions.

Teamwork is also featured in online games, especially those involving more than one player on each side. Participants are able to come together and achieve a common goal to win the game. In doing that, they formulate and carry out strategies, brainstorming towards their common end. The discipline imbibed from working with others, following authority, and sticking to a plan go a long way in developing the child's skills for similar challenges in the physical world.

Socializing

Facebook is probably the first platform to come to mind when mention is made of Social Media. Yet, this very popular platform that has made its founder the youngest billionaire in the world, did not come into existence until 2004, more than a decade after the Internet went public. Yahoo and MySpace had been very popular with user of the Internet until Facebook came onto the scene and changed the face of online socializing forever.

There are different kinds of "Social Media", ranging from general ones like Facebook, Twitter, Internet forums etc. to professional ones like LinkedIn. These platforms have similar features in the design, including sharing textual information as well as multimedia files like photos, audios and videos. Another feature built into these platforms is instant messaging, which allows users to send and receive messages instantly, i.e. chat. This last feature has been the sole purpose of other platforms like WhatsApp, BlackBerry Messenger, Telegram, Facebook Messenger, iMessage, Signal, Threema etc.

Most online gaming platforms have the chat feature built in (as well as a voice-chat-feature), too, and allow participants to interact with one another during games. This way, people of different origins, races and creeds are united by a common cause: gaming and having fun together. Other details can be exchanged and relationships can transcend only gaming, and can last for a lifetime.

Fun

There is so much fun to have on the Internet. With video platforms like YouTube and other social media platforms like Facebook, Instagram, Pinterest, Twitter, and so on users have unlimited access to resources for sharing information. Therefore, it is not surprising that memes (a term for images with captions) and fun videos have become so commonplace that the channels through which they are offered command thousands of followers or subscribers (making it possible to earn money with it). Similarly, audio information is shared in the form of podcasts and other users can subscribe to your feed in order to follow your posts.

Online gaming is only one of the many types of fun you can have online. It can be resorted to when you need to have a nice time with a friend, and even family. You can keep your children engaged with it, and even use it to develop a healthy competition amongst them. And what's even more fun about it is the flexibility with which it can be accessed. With a smartphone and just about any platform, such as Telegram, you can keep your children busy with trivia bots and possibly add some reward to it for good performance.

Additional Opportunities

From what has been said so far about the Internet, you can conclude that a door of opportunities were opened because it was unrestricted to the public and its commercialization. Nowadays, it is not uncommon to find online stores where you can order goods and services and have it delivered to you online and offline in the shortest time possible. But, the opportunities available on the Internet go beyond just commercial ones.

On some platforms, employers are busy scouting for the *right* employees. Communities are organizing competitions for persons of various ages and fields, hoping to reward talents and create paths to stardom. Such competitions may border on games, essay writing, arts, crafts, science and technology, and others, etc. With proper guidance, you can get your children to participate in and guide them through the process, starting from the instructions through the preparation of entries to their submission. This way, your children can win scholarships, relieving you of some of the financial responsibilities for their continued education. They can also be rewarded with trips abroad, participation in some international or national conferences where they meet new people and gain access to even more opportunities.

- **The Bad**

Bullying is a common thing in every school, especially elementary and high schools. but since everything has gone online, so has bullying. In fact, victims of online bullying are not limited to children or young people, but adults, too. Bullying takes place on any platform where people interact with one another, and the effects of online bullying can be just as much as suffering from it offline, if not greater. This will become clearer when you consider the fixed nature of content online. A bullying reply or post on an online forum can always be there as reference for people to see, which is something that is not possible offline.

Recalling that online games have forums and chatting features built into them, these are avenues for bullying. Participants usually assume anonymous names online, but it is not uncommon to find participants revealing their true identities on other platforms when boasting of their exploits in the gaming community. This, in essence, removes the cloak of anonymity and the victim of cyber-bullying is known for all to see.

Data volumes and purchases

As games today contain more and more data, the amount of data that has to be transferred for games has exploded. Especially for mobile games on smartphones which do not have a "data-flatrate", costs can arise that need to be kept in mind.

Another cost factor can be the purchase of virtual goods. Many game manufacturers today live from purchasing of additional content within the game ("in-app-purchase"), as the games themselves are often made available free of charge. It is obvious that children in particular like to react to such advertised content and pay real money for virtual goods.

Distraction

Distraction can be a bad effect of online gaming for so many reasons. Considering the fact that participants are located in different parts of the world and, in effect, in different time zones, Jill may be online when Jack is supposed to be asleep or when Anne is busy with her homework. With the designing of gaming gadgets and smartphones, push notifications allow other participants who are not online to get updates on the activities of those that are online. The problem, therefore, lies in such notifications coming in at the wrong time and the participant who is offline is distracted from more important, real life matters.

It is equally possible for the participant to get easily distracted by his thoughts of having to be online at a specific time he or she knows others would be online. Such an instance as this and the other earlier one mentioned can lead to divided attention, causing the child to spend less time on other, more important engagements. Of course, this also applies to normal chatting via a mobile phone without a game reference.

Restricted Contents

Certain resources online may not necessarily be meant for children, and thus they are restricted. Different things are put into consideration when deciding who should have access to certain things, and one of them is violence. Game designers always want games to be a replica of things in the real world so some of their content may be considered inappropriate for certain ages. The Internet itself, however, offers ways of getting access to adult content, as all it takes is an Internet search, or asking someone who knows.

> The vast majority (87%) of youth who report looking for sexual images online are 14 years of age or older![9]

Wrong Information

Since the information explosion following the opening of the Internet to the public in the 1990s, one problem that has arisen is the appearance of wrong information, or "fake news". Powerful search engines such as Google return information considered most relevant to the search terms to the users, notwithstanding their correctness. The user is, therefore, left with the task of determining the truth or falsehood of the information presented. Though this may be relatively easy for experienced users and adults, it is problematic for kids. Such platforms where incorrect information can be easily picked up are Social Media-channels, blogs and forums. Many 'internet journalists' have also taken to inspiring and creating fake news content on the web in a bid to attract web traffic and clicks, which in turn generates revenue for advertisement.

- **The Ugly**

Having discussed the bad side of the Internet, we now turn to discuss the ugly side of it, which goes beyond the simple effects of its distraction and the access to pornographic sites.

Pornography

Pornographic websites are one of the most visited places on the Internet. There are literally millions of them and new ones are cropping up on a daily basis. Web browsers also allow users to easily visit these sites without leaving a trail. The possibility of children accessing pornographic contents does not arise when the game is being played through desktop applications, or gaming gadgets. It arises when the game is being played through web browsers that do not have parental restrictions on what sites the child can access.

Terrorism

When people say everything that's good has a negative side, they cannot be more right when the statement is considered in the context of terrorism and the Internet. While there are opportunities to make money, attain stardom, contribute to the peace and development of humanity online, there are opportunities to unleash terror on others by destroying computer-based information systems for the purpose of injuring, instilling fear, or causing loss to others. This act of terrorism is known as cyber-terrorism.

However, considering that terrorism is based on ideologies, and ideologies need humans to survive, there is the need for terrorist organizations to recruit new members. Since the Internet offers anonymity, security and privacy, it is the darling tool of the terrorists to recruit new converts. Such recruitment exercises are done stealthily online..

Internet Fraud

Internet fraud is another ugly side of the Internet that has become commonplace. A good many people have lost substantial amounts of money to it. In fact, so many *still* lose money to it. The temptation is the allure of making an incredible amount of money with very little investment. There is a risk of meeting a potential fraudster on any platform on the Internet. They are in forums, chat groups, Facebook groups, Google circles, LinkedIn connection, in the gaming community etc.

Since an adult can play games meant for children, children playing online games can be coaxed or tricked by such fraudsters to reveal the confidential details of their parents, such as credit card information. The bait can be anything from selling cheat codes to unlocking higher levels of an online game. This only presents you and your child as the victim. Nothing says platforms cannot be used to coax your child into committing fraud or into being an accessory to such a crime.

Other Cybercrimes

There are other cybercrimes. One of such crime is the illegal download of media content from the internet, a crime which has become widespread in recent times due to the development of new shielding technologies like virtual private networks that disguise the true location of a person accessing the protected file without proper authorization. Almost any digital product sold online can be obtained through many other platforms at no cost at all other than cellular data.

Ideas about how to and where to download such files are shared on various online platforms such as private chat groups, forums, blogs, private chats etc.

Internet-based gaming: Pros and Cons

One of the crucial roles of the Internet lies in the social networking of people, as a result of which they can share information. This networking feature has been introduced to the gaming world, where, through an Internet connection, co-gamers can now interact with one another.

Games that have this inherent feature are called online games, and are usually partially or completely dependent upon an Internet connection. Online games have become popular over the years across several gaming platforms, starting primarily in computers and spreading to game consoles, mobiles phones and handhelds, which all require the internet. The design of online games can range from simple text-based environments to the incorporation of complex graphics and virtual worlds. The existence of online components within a game can range from being minor features, such as an online leaderboard, to being part of core gameplay, such as directly playing against other players (e.g. MMORPG - Massively multiplayer online role-playing games). Many online games create their own online communities, while other games, especially "social games", integrate the players' existing real-life communities into the virtual world.

Online games offer a lot of benefits, including cognitive development, de-stressing, and entertainment. They also promote communication and teamwork through their inherent social aspects. Providing people an incentive to work with each other to win at games helps them interact better with others at their school- and workspaces or in their day-to-day lives offline. This is especially helpful for introverts, as it allows them to communicate with other people through a medium that is more tangibly under their control. This can enable them to get more comfortable with interpersonal interactions. However, as most online games support an in-game chat function, it is not uncommon to encounter hate speech, sexual harassment and cyberbullying. Given the potential for a number of unwanted scenarios — predators have been known to use this gateway to try to groom potential victims — parents must explain the risks their children can be exposed to, and ask that they only play with approved peers. Clear rules are required here (more about this in the next chapters).

To make the benefits derived from online gaming outweigh the potential harms, parents must make certain to educate and guide their young ones in the use of online gaming platforms. For instance, bearing in mind that most online games require players to create an 'account' before playing, parents should advise children to always use aliases when filling in parts that require their names. Parents in regards to the internet should establish clear and strict rules! These false names should not be a derivative of, or give information about, the child's real name (and passwords), and should generally differ across different gaming platforms. Another issue of concern is the privacy and security threats posed by hackers. Hackers have been proven to be able to have access to, and therefore control, certain parts of computers and other internet-accessing devices, such as webcams. This illicitly obtained footage can be used to intimidate or blackmail parents and children, alike. To help put this risk in check, make sure to scan the system of your children for virus and malware regularly, to update them with new software, and to ensure that all of your device's webcam and microphones is set to "off". A new threat is in the use of "voice chats". In games like *Fortnite,* players all over the world can gather in teams and speak freely using microphone equipment. This voice chat functionality is not new and was employed by games in the past for an older target group. It is important that younger kids get informed not to give any private information to strangers over voice chats.

In 2018, fortnite became the most successful free-to-play game ever with over 125 million players around the world

In addition, make sure you are the one sanctioning all mobile and WLAN downloads and purchases using real money.Make sure to play your role by talking to your children about these risks.

STATUS OF SCIENTIFIC RESEARCH_

THIS CHAPTER FOCUSES on the results of scientific studies that have been conducted in the area of game-based learning for children, and highlights the benefits of judicious use of gaming devices and the dangers in overusing them.

In 2003, James Paul Gee [10] published a research article titled "What Video Games Have to Teach Us about Learning and Literacy" that detailed how games can help shape the approach of kids to being taught. In the decade that followed, James' work was cited more than 5,000 times. Broadly, there are three major ideas of how to approach the research in the field of game-based-learning.

The first approachsees the topic as a form of approach to learning driven by games and gaming technologies. This point of view states that by playing games, students are helping to develop their intellectual abilities more, to enable them to cope better with their studies. This school of thought believes that introducing students to games can aid in the learning process and can be smoother and more efficient. If anything, it seeks to clarify that games actually offer help to students. Therefore, by playing games, students better equip their brain to work better during formal learning.

The second approach sees game-based learning as a learning approach that should also include pedagogies. The idea is to construct games around learning activities in such a way that it becomes more interesting and easy to follow for the participants. Under the tutelage of a teacher, students can essentially use games to sharpen their focus and to improve their knowledge. It essentially asks that games be fused into formal education as a means of better explanation.

The third approach sees game based learning as a pedagogical innovation informed by game design principles. This school of thought views concepts such as role-playing and a completion and reward system as essential in the act of learning while gaming. Squire, (2004) [11] posited that when participants play complex problem-solving games, they may learn new insights in real life problem solving. That means that kids, and even adults, exposed to games subconsciously imbibe some of the skills that they apply to game situations.

In May 2012, SRI International and Glass Lab, released the result of two meta-analyses on simulations and game-based learning. In the first report titled "Digital Games for Learning", the showed evidence that relative to other instruction condition, digital games showed significant positive effects on science, math, and literacy outcomes. The design of the games plays an important role in the success achieved in learning.

As postulated by Siegler and Ramani (2008), [12] it is also quite possible that "a lack of skills in the use of numbers among children from low-income households might be due to their limited opportunities to play number games during their childhood." This is true for traditional games as well as video games. Electronic games games offer an alternative and ultimately a more exciting way to learn abstract contents and mathematical relationships.

Liu and Chen, (2013) [13] also demonstrated that card games can help improve factual knowledge-gaining abilities and arouse genuine interest in the learning among students. Their study used a card game, "Conveyance-Go", to demonstrate that students assimilate information faster when an element of gaming is coupled with the learning process. At the end of their study, the subjects showed a faster grasp of transportation and energy systems compared to a more conventionally bland approach. Pre-test and post-test results showed that the game significantly raised the knowledge level of the study participants.

Digital games are an effective way of de-stressing and getting away from the tiring, tasking daily activities that wear us out. Gaming has been proven by studies [14][15][16] to be beneficial to the human mind and especially to that of a child as it grows and develops. There are studies [17][18], however, that also point out the negative effects that arise as a result of over-indulgence in video games. It is a sufficient statement that gaming is a double-edged sword and can cut both ways – in this case it may either cut and relieve stress, or cut and reduce the mind's power and capability. A clear consensus about the advantages and the disadvantages is not yet found. Therefore, as espoused by the conclusions of several scientific studies conducted under varying conditions and different climes, games have a great potential in aiding the dissemination of information to students in a faster, more efficient way. However, the study situation – especially in the field of game based learning- is still poor.

The Concept of Game-Based Learning

The idea of using games to engage children in the process of active learning is not new. Over the past several years, educators have been increasingly incorporating various games into their teaching curriculum in an effort to create a fun and engaging learning environment for students. Although this can be very challenging and time consuming, interactive, collaborative and competitive games tend to motivate and encourage student participation in the learning process. In his research, Marzano [19] explains that of the 60 studies he has been involved in, the effects of games on student achievement, "on average, using academic games in the classroom is associated with a 20 percentile point gain in student achievement".

There are many explanations as to what defines an "educational game" nowadays. While some games are competitive in nature, others may simply allow students to work together as a class to solve a general problem where no one "wins" or "loses." Educational games have been broadly grouped under two main categories of media-based and non-media based games. Media-based educational games are those that are designed for, and essentially carried out on, electronic gadgets such as mobile phones, laptops, gaming consoles, and tablets. Non-media educational games, on the other hand, are such games as board and interactive classroom games, which can be infused with educational information, so as to impart knowledge on players. Regardless of the category of games, game-based learning has been proven [20] to partially have profound effects on children's cognitive and problem solving skills. In the technological context, there are many computer-based games that provide active learning opportunities and reinforce topics learned in the classroom. It must be stated though, that these games are not using modern technologies and useful gaming elements enough in order to create an exciting gaming experience. One important aspect for educators to consider when employing these games is the way in which they arrange for players to interact with the game and their co-players. They can work independently and compete against the computer, or play together with other player in the classroom to promote cooperative learning. In general, games played in teams have been found [21] to enhance academic achievement and attitudes towards the subject matter taught by the games.

PART TWO:_

SAILING THROUGH THE CHAOS

WHY YOU SHOULD ENCOURAGE GAMING_

IN THIS CHAPTER, we will shift to the reasons why you, as a parent, need to encourage your child to play educational games and to use the functionalities of online collaboration . This chapter discusses the importance of games in a child's growth and development. For the purpose of clarity, the reasons have been divided into three major groups: social, mental and intellectual. Each of these is further subdivided into smaller manageable points. It is to these that I now turn.

Social Reasons

It is virtually impossible for anyone to live alone and not interact with other people, even if such a person were mute. Communication is an important feature of human societies; it is the very basis of our organization into society. Through communication, ideas are exchanged, opinions weighed and preferred or dropped. The social reasons why you should encourage your child's participation in online gaming relate to the child's interaction with others, and his or her participation as a member of society. It is the importance of social interactions that led to the development of social media, which now allow people of the most diverse origins to come together and interact, to compare and even form greater bonds that transcend their geographical and national borders.

• **Improves Social Interaction**

One of the advantages of online gaming is that it improves social interaction among children and between children and older persons. Online gaming provides a common interest on which two people can interact. Realizing you and someone else play the same game can be the beginning of a friendship, just as people who read the same type of book can get along more easily in conversations. Why? There is always something to talk about, ranging from the things they enjoy in the game to strategies and the things they dislike about the game.

• **Connections and Networks**

A point closely linked to the first is the possibility of creating connections and maintaining a network of such. It should not be surprising that online gaming can bring your child new friends and acquaintances. These bonds may be sufficient reason for some people to prefer you, to some other, in instances where such persons have the liberty to choose as they wish. It can even go beyond personal relations and into business ones. For example, people who have interest in a common game may decide to team up and start their own studio to design similar games. In fact, companies of young people that have earned quite amount of money have already been created in this way.

Mental and cognitive reasons

The second set of reasons why you should encourage your child to participate in online gaming can be put into the mental and cognitive category (i.e. relating to the development of his or her brain capabilities). In this regard, two benefits of online gaming come to mind and are discussed below.

- **Hand-eye Coordination**

. Our brains control most of the things our bodies do.

To excel at certain activities, however, we must develop a pattern of action or some type of unnatural ability i.e. ability which we do not ordinarily possess from birth. A good example is driving or typing on the computer. In both of these cases, you need your fingers and eyes to work in perfect synchronization or else you might have to pay an ultimate penalty in the case of driving, or you might have to lose so much time from having to go back to correct typographical errors in the case of typing.

However, engaging in activities that require the use of the hands and the eyes simultaneously will help improve just how much you can get these two important organs to work in sync. This is where gaming comes in. Whether online or offline, it can improve hand-eye coordination, although this is not true for all games. It is, however, true for most games that requires the use of pads or joysticks..

- **Memory Enhancement**

Some other types of games may not help improve your hand-eye coordination, but they are most certainly busy improving another important aspect of your cognition: memory. Memory is at the heart of our cognition. Not only does it define time itself but also communication. Our brain needs to be able to match the sound waves it's receiving from the outside, with the familiar signs, and then call the meanings attached to such sound. For example, when you hear someone exclaim 'Run, Fire!' your brain has to process these two words and then kick you into action. It is, however, only able to do that because it has retained the meaning of those words. This same process goes for seeing, feeling, tasting, and more. In fact, intelligence, too, depends on having a good memory.

Quiz Trivia and a host of board games are what come to mind when we speak of games improving memory. One of the reasons why we forget things is the low frequency of our interaction with those things. This is why you probably won't remember most of what happens in the novel you read about a year ago. Quiz Trivia may trigger pieces of information here and there, and that way your brain tries to create the whole connection again. A host of other games are designed specifically to help strengthen the human capacity to recollect information.

Intellectual Reasons

Intellectual in this case means Hence, critical thinking, creative thinking, and a robust knowledge base.

- **Critical Thinking for Problem Solving**

This is an intellectual activity that relies on the use of the brain to arrive at a sound judgment. Critical thinking may require research and possession of a knowledge base with which to compare and contrast ideas or opinions. It is the ability to reason logically and analytically, however, it is not something that we are born with. It is something that is taught or learned over time and with practice.

Some games are specifically designed to teach this while others teach the skill incidentally. Consider chess. To be able to excel at the game of chess, you need to be able to think critically and analytically, to be able to anticipate the possible moves of your opponent and think up counter-moves for each possible move. Chess is not the only game in this category as there are other games (As strategy games or simulations) designed specifically to train the brain (or certain parts of it) to be able to smoothly achieve certain tasks.

- **Creative Thinking**

Creative thinking is quite different from critical thinking. This difference becomes clear when you understand that it is possible to score high on an IQ test and not be able to handle new situations. Yes, new situations! The keyword is new, or the idea of novelty. When someone can think creatively, then they can combine old ideas, related or unrelated, experience insights, and come up with something new. Creative thinking strikes at the heart of creativity, whether in the sciences or the arts.

Leonardo Da Vinci was one of the prominent figures in history to fully utilize creative thinking. Before he died, he left schematics for several new inventions without himself in fact designing a good lot of them. When later others followed his plans, the needed results were achieved. Creative thinking is what's common to both Darwin and Babbage apart from the two having 'Charles' as their first names. Darwin saw a different pattern in the fossil records and came up with the theory of evolution. Babbage is regarded as the father of the modern computer, not because he designed a working model, but because he laid a plan and theory to follow that still works till date. Einstein's story may not be very much different when his theory of relativity is considered.

Games have the ability to induce new insights, new ideas. Some games offer the possibility to create completely new games or levels (e.g. Game Maker, Construct, Game Salad, RPG Maker, Mario Maker, Unity 3D and other engines, etc.). In fact, some games usually require you to think completely out of the box in order to arrive at solutions. Playing such games over a period of time may be just the needed practice for getting adept at a particular method of thought, and it may not be long before your child starts applying such a skill to real life events.

- **Robust Knowledgebase**

Knowledge, however, is the understanding of the content of information, and how the pieces, thereof, relate to one another. It is the clarity and clear awareness possessed about a situation or fact.

You might be thinking Quiz Trivia is the only type of game that can help improve your knowledge base. There are learning games of all sort, which improve knowledge, from crossword puzzles to business simulations.

YOUR ROLE IN YOUR CHILD'S GAME-BASED LEARNING_

PLAYING video games has garnered a lot of negative reputation, especially from older people, or parents, who feel that time spent playing on gaming devices is valuable time wasted. Although there are ounces of truth underlying this notion, it may not be entirely true.

Video games have become an established part of life in the modern world, and more so in young people. A study conducted by the NPD shows that approximately 91% of children in the U.S. between the ages of 2 and 17 years play video games across several digital platforms and devices including smartphones, tablets, laptops, and gaming consoles. More interesting, these numbers are up nearly 13 percent from a 2009 study [47]. Gaming among kids between 2 and 5 years has increased the most. Games played on mobile devices alone, the study adds, have risen from 8 percent to 38 percent. Android and iOS devices account for most of the growth. Games played on handheld systems like the Nintendo 3DS are up from 38 percent to 45 percent since 2009.

How You Can Help

Caught in the quagmire of having to decide whether gaming is good or harmful for their children, parents and teachers are often left sadly confused, and even more sadly, without other options than to indulge in destructive permissiveness or harsh restriction. Showing an indifferent attitude towards your child's gaming life is an easy, but harmful thing to do. Different aspects have to be considered. For instance, depending on the age and developmental stage of the child, some gaming content is regarded as inappropriate for kids and should not be consumed by them. Exposure to inappropriate content can severely harm a child's emotional and psychological wellbeing. That is not to say that restricting your kids from engaging with video games altogether is the solution, as some of these games can play vital roles in the cognitive and intellectual development of children (as seen in the last chapters).

So, what can you do as a parent? There are many expert opinions out there about how parents can cope with the issue of children gaming and how they can maintain a reasonable stronghold on their kids' gaming experience. Due to the lag of common agreements, some of these opinions agree on specific aspects and disagree on others. A very problematic point is the fact that most studies do focus on media usage and "normal" games and not educational games and their influence.

It is worthy to pointy out that the area of gaming for children is still mostly unexamined by scientific research, therefore, you're not going to get any concrete laws or principles as to what to do as a parent or how to do it. However, these expert opinions have been able to alleviate the confusion in parents as to whether they should allow their children to play games or forbid them totally, by pointing out the beneficial and harmful aspects of gaming. The following applies in any case: A wide knowledge of what is good and what is bad about video games gives you a strong footing in determining what games you want your children to engage with. These opinions have also, to a large extent, shined light on the clouded subject of game time for kids.

Experts advise that children who are old enough to want to play video games should be encouraged to do so. According to child and adolescent psychologist Belén Mata [22] at the Austral University Hospital in Argentina, "video games don't, as such, pose an intrinsic risk to children: it depends on the particular content and the use they make of them". This assertion suggests that the act of playing video games in itself is not wrong. What can pose risks of adverse effects is the *content* of these games and time spent on it. Extrinsic effects (such as lag of movement and social isolation) must be added though. She further explains the dependency of gaming in regards to the age of the children: "Young children need parents to explain the contents of what they are viewing, so as to think about and understand them". This is to say, early on, children require the guidance of parents to make them better conceptualize what it is they're doing. Mata goes on to give some guidelines on parent-to-child gaming guidance, which include accompanying them in playing games, setting healthy limits, and making use of resources designed to help consumers make informed decisions when buying video games or apps. Similar guidelines were published by many governments and institutes over the world (e.g. Child Mind Institute, American Academy of Pediatrics etc.).

Furthermore, you must be aware of your roles and responsibilities to your child outside of gaming. You could develop alternatives to playing video games during their spare time by encouraging them to indulge in activities that can help bolster their physical and mental health outside the world of video games. As stated by family physicians Camila Giménez and Celeste Berecoechea at the Austral University Hospital, "the role of adults is crucial in developing alternatives (to video games), creating shared activities that can acquire a special meaning for all parties involved. Activities such as cooking or doing chores together, family games and sports, going for a walk, engaging in word games and fostering reading habits, can all become appealing activities to a child if an adult is involved."

Recognizing the inability of younger persons, at least a majority of them, to make good judgments for themselves, manufacturers, inventors, designers, and service providers usually build parental-control features into their products. Such features are in place to help you as a parent. In the succeeding subsections of this chapter, some of these features will be discussed.

Placing Restrictions

This topic is addressed under the following headings: electronic restrictions, Internet restrictions, physical restrictions, use of schedules, and monitoring activities and using filters.

1. **Electronic Restrictions**

- **Restrictions on Phones and Tablets**

Smartphones and tablets, or handheld devices in general, come with parental control features. This feature allows the parent to determine what the child will have access to while using the device. For example, a parent can determine which apps their child can access, and what settings they can change when operating the phone. Examples of this feature can be found in the iOS 'screen time' functionality and Android's digital wellbeing functionality.

You can restrict your kids' gaming using simple rules!

There are also third party applications (e.g. KIDOZ: Safe Mode) that can create further restrictions, or even alert parents when the barriers they set for their children are transgressed. Such apps can be downloaded and installed from the respective app store for the various devices.

- **Restrictions on PCs**

Everything that has been said so far about parental-control on phones also applies to parental control on personal computers. Parental control software can be installed on almost any computer a child has access to. One simple way on Windows to restrict your child's access to files and apps is to use the guest account feature. That way, you can keep the password to the main account on the system a secret.

You can also set restrictions on what websites your children can access when they are using the web browsers installed on the computer. This you can do using plugins or add-ons designed by third parties. You should be aware that children can be smart enough to Google ways of bypassing such restrictions, so you should always try to foresee such ways and put in place appropriate measures. An example of the restriction functionalities available on PCs is the Windows 10 screen time functionality. For MacOS there is the parental control function, and certain Linux-GUIs offer similar possibilities.

- **Restrictions on Gaming Consoles**

First and foremost, always remember to look at the ratings on games. In the US, the ESRB is the ratings board that determines the appropriate audience for a game and sets a rating much like the MPAA does for films. The ESRB has an easy to use website, www.esrb.org, where you can look up ratings by title and break down what different content tags mean. Some consoles offer an age restriction function which is build into the system. Beyond that, making sure that consoles are set up correctly to enable (or disable) certain functions — like web browsing, voice chat, and store purchases — is the other crucial aspect to ensuring their security.

Below is a breakdown of how to set up parental control restrictions on different gaming devices including Nintendo Wii U, Nintendo 3DS,

PlayStation 4, and Xbox One.

Nintendo Switch & Wii U

Nintendo is well known for being a family-friendly company, and the parental controls options for their Wii U console are robust, varied, and very easy to enable. First off, while the Wii U has network functions like online multiplayer, chat, and an online store, these features are disabled for users under 12 (which is determined when a user account is first set up by inputting their age). In the instance of a user being too young to access network functions, parents may choose to consent to letting their child use these functions by accepting the consent agreement and paying a non-refundable $0.50 (this is to ensure that parents know that online functions have been enabled via an alert on their bank account statement).

If you opted in to network functionality and still wish to set up privacy and content settings for your child, you will need to create a PIN and secret answer for a security question that you will use to access these options. This is to prevent your child from changing it on their own.

In order to access these settings, simply go to the Wii U menu and select Parental Controls. After inputting your PIN, you may make changes to permissions for the following content:

- Restrict game access by rating (e.g. using Pegi.info)
- In-game chat
- Wii-U chat
- Miiverse (Nintendo's console-based social media network)
- Friends
- Online store
- Web browser use and settings
- Data management (i.e. deletion or copying of data on the system, such as save game data and downloaded program

data)
- Non-gaming apps, like Netflix or YouTube

With the Nintendo Switch parental controls, you can, among other things, limit gaming times in a similar way, even day-by-day. Statistics provide information about the most played games. Here too, games can be automatically blocked due to age restrictions. The same applies to online and social media functions.

Nintendo 3DS

To enable parental controls on a 3DS system, begin by pressing the HOME button and tapping the System Settings button that pops up. From here, tap Parental Controls, and follow the on-screen steps. You will be asked to create a four-digit PIN, and input an email address. The email will be used as a contact in order to reset your PIN if it is forgotten. Once you've completed the setup, head back to the HOME menu by, once again, selecting Parental Controls. You are now able to change the parental control settings. (Note: these steps are consistent across all versions of the Nintendo 3DS hardware, including the 3DS, 3DS XL, 2DS, and the new 3DS).

On the 3DS, there are the follow options:

- Restrict game access by rating
- Communication with Friends
- Miiverse (Nintendo's console-based social media network)
- Restrictions for the Chat
- Restrictions for the e-Shop store
- Restrictions for the Apps
- Restrictions for the Web browser
- Restrictions for the Street Pass (a wi-fi based connectivity feature that allows systems to trade characters, called Miis,

back and forth, even while the system is closed)
- Settings for 3D image display

PlayStation 4

In order to set up parental controls on a PS4, first begin by creating a Master Account for yourself, and Sub Account(s) for your children. You can do this when you first set up the console, or by going to the PSN options on the console menu and following the on-screen instructions to create a new account. Once you have a Master Account set up, you can now create a sub account. To do this, sign in to your master account, and then follow these steps:

1. Navigate to the settings menu, and select Parental Controls.
2. In this menu, find and select Sub Accounts Management. You will be asked to input your PSN username and password.
3. Next, select Create Sub Account. You will be given an explanation of Sub Accounts, and the system will take you through the steps to set up your child's account.

Once you've created your Sub Account(s), navigate back to the System Menu, to Parental Controls, and from there you can access a number of options to set for each Sub Account, including:

- Restricting games, apps, DVDs and Blue-Rays by their age rating
- Disabling/Enabling the use of the PS4 web browser
- Restricting non-registered user logins
- Disabling messages to and from other PSN users
- Setting spending limits on the PlayStation Store
- Blocking content on the PlayStation Store

Xbox One

On a single Xbox One console, multiple accounts of varying types can be stored and shared by setting up a Family Profile. To do this, press the Menu button on your Xbox One controller. Select Settings and scroll to Family. From here, you can manage the accounts within your Xbox's family; add or remove accounts to/from the family (this does not affect an account's ability to use the console); and change settings. Account types range from adult, to teen, to child, and each type has its own restrictions and permissions when it comes to changing settings or accessing content:

- Adult accounts have no restrictions. They are able to play any movie or game, access online features, as well as make changes to the system settings, and settings on teen or child accounts on the system.
- Teen accounts, by default, do not have many restrictions; games, movies, and online features are available. However, these permissions can all be changed by an adult account.
- Child accounts (suggested for users eight years old and under), have pre-set restrictions to content use by rating, and limited online functions available. These settings can be changed by adult accounts.

Once a family profile has been created, you may now create privacy settings for each account. To do so, once again navigate to the Settings menu by pressing Menu on the controller, and then selecting Family. Once there, you may select a profile to edit.

- **Internet-Based Restrictions**

Internet restrictions can also be employed to limit gaming on electronic devices and is achieved by configuring your Internet router so that it limits the data usage or implies time limits. This method of restriction can be used to restrict gaming across several platforms – such as PCs, smartphones, TV and consoles –, simultaneously.

- **Physical Restrictions**

The discussion about restriction so far has only covered electronic restrictions. Physical restrictions are another option. You can lock the game console away in your closet when school is in session and bring it out only during the holidays or weekends. You can decide whether or not your children should take their phones to school with them or not. You can equally monitor their access to other ways of getting access to online games.

1. **Use of Schedules**

Total restriction cannot work for some games, especially the educative ones such as quiz trivia. So, what matters most is *scheduled* access to prevent them from distracting your child at inopportune times. You need to factor your child's schedule into yours, so you have to create the opportunity for your child to be able to play the game, though on your terms, and always keep to the schedule. In fact, to ensure games do not interfere with your kid's academic performance, you should make additional game time a reward for extra effort put into the academic activities at school or subtract gaming time if agreements are not met.

Another way of scheduling game time is by drafting a timetable to stipulate the amount of time, per day, that your child can spend on their computer. Stipulated times may be purposefully made to be lopsided, granting less screen time on Mondays, Tuesdays, Wednesdays, Thursdays and Sundays, and more on Fridays, Saturdays and holidays.

The key to taking back control of the media in your home is to make agreements ahead of time - before the TV or computer ever turns on. There should be a clear agreement that spells out the limits and rules about the use of the game. Here's what it might look like (bear in mind that this table has been made specific to a number of children, but should still be useful across many family structures):

Days	Time	Platform			
		Nintendo	Mobile	TV	Computer
Monday	4-5pm	Mike			
Tuesday	4-5pm		Mike		
Wednesday	4-5pm	Day off			
Thursday	4-5pm			Mike	
Friday	3-6pm	Mike		Mike	
Saturday	3-6pm	Mike	Mike		Mike
Sunday	3-5pm		Mike	Mike	Mike

Table 7.1: An example schedule of game engagement for Mike (12 years old, with good grades)

Days	Time	Platform			
		PlayStation	Tablet	TV	Computer
Monday					
Tuesday					
Wednesday					
Thursday					
Friday					
Saturday	3 hours max	Cindy	Cindy	Cindy	Cindy
Sunday	2 hours max	Cindy	Cindy	Cindy	Cindy

Table 7.2: An example schedule of game engagement for Cindy (10, with not so good grades)

Days	Time	Platform			
		PlayStation	Tablet	TV	Computer Educational Games
Monday					Educational game
Tuesday			Educational game		
Wednesday					
Thursday					Educational game
Friday			Educational game		
Saturday	3 hours max	Cindy	Cindy	Cindy	Cindy
Sunday	2 hours max	Cindy	Cindy	Cindy	Cindy

Table 7.3: An example schedule of game engagement to help Cindy in school subjects (10, with not so good grades)

Another option is to let kids decide, on their own terms, which device to use as long as it falls within the stipulated maximum amount of time. A third option is to manage a time contingent, e.g. based on good school grades (every time a kid gets a good grade, extra time is added to the stipulated time). The options for scheduling game time and platform are near endless and depend mostly on the kids themselves, their interests, school grades, and the level of trust you have in them as their parents.

The all-important agreement is that they must understand the agreement *before* they turn on the game. Then it must be hung up on the refrigerator or somewhere visible. That way, if a kid is trying to go off-limits, or if there is a fight over whose turn it is, anyone can refer to the written schedule. If they do not adhere to their agreement, than the system is off for the day. This is a great way to implement healthy restrictions on gaming. Generally, it is important that parents promote the use of good educational games and prefer them to any other form of games!

- **Monitoring Activities and Using Filters**

Monitoring the activities of your children online is very important for several reasons. A quick example is that you wouldn't want your child making racist posts on Facebook, would you? Therefore, monitoring your child's activities online, especially in the gaming communities online, is extremely important. As the parent and guardian of your children, you have some room to intrude into their privacy by accepting their privacy on the one hand but taking care of your responsibilities on the other. Places you could check include your web browser's history, the messages exchanged between your children and other people, and the downloads folder. It might also be useful to let the kids explain the websites it used or the posts it wrote.

The use of filter mechanisms (see point B) that prevent inappropriate content might also be a good solution for kids of younger ages. These filters can be configured so that certain Internet addresses and keywords are blocked (this is especially important if the children have free access to sites such as YouTube, or any other media streaming website). Prohibiting kids from the abililty to make online payments is also highly advisable. How often do the news tell stories about kids ordering expensive stuff using Amazon Echo's or other devices?

This may require effort and commitment, but you can be rest assured that it is all worth it. It is better to nip any funny plan your children might have or might have been exposed to in the bud rather than see them face the consequences. In some instances, monitoring might save you, too. While your child may not be able to tell that he or she is being coaxed into revealing your confidential information, you as an adult will be able to spot it with very little, or no efforts at all.

Dealing with Video Game Addiction

Though lacking a single, generalized definition, many experts have described video game addiction, or simply VGA, as a form of behavioral addiction characterized by excessive or compulsive use of computer games or video games that interferes with a person's everyday life. The disorder may present as compulsive indulgence in gaming, social isolation, mood swings, plummeted imagination, and exaggerated focus on in-game virtual achievements, to the exclusion of other events in life. In its 11th International Classification of Diseases (ICD-11), the World Health Organization (WHO) listed VGA as a mental health disorder requiring medical intervention.

The cardinal difference between a healthy gaming life and an addiction lies in the distinctive characteristics of video game addiction, which are stated by the WHO as: impaired control over the desire for gaming, increasing priority given to gaming to the extent that gaming takes precedence over other life interests and daily activities, and continuation or escalation of gaming despite the occurrence of negative consequences. That is to say, people – including children – can have an enthusiastic gaming attitude without, in this case, being an addict. In fact, this point is evident in the fact that out of all the millions of gamers worldwide, about 3 – 4% are estimated to have VGA. The reasons why one person develops VGA and others do not are unknown. Playing games has nothing to do with it – it is the result, not the origin. As in many mental disorders, the problems originate in many aspects, which go beyond the topic of this book.

The hazards of video game addiction range from mild effects like sleep disorders, moodiness, irritation, and malnourishment due to poor dieting, to severe effects including depression, physical aggression, agoraphobia (a disorder characterized by fear of leaving the house), and hikikomori (a Japanese term given to an adolescent's withdrawal from social life). These effects have been found to exacerbate with time, and could potentially destroy a child's hope for a healthy life.

You can do this by watching out for the following signs and symptoms of VGA:

1. Intensive preoccupation with video games. If your child only thinks about previous gaming activity or anticipates playing the next game, there's a chance they're addicted.
2. Showing withdrawal symptoms when gaming is taken away. These symptoms are typically described as irritability, anxiety, boredom, cravings, or sadness.
3. Loss of interests in previous hobbies and entertainment as a result of, and with the exception of, video games.
4. The need to spend increasing amounts of time engaged in video games.
5. Has jeopardized or lost an important relationship, hobbies, school grades, job, educational, or career opportunity because of indulgence in video games.
6. Continued excessive participation in video gaming despite knowledge of psychosocial effects, and unsuccessful attempts to control engagement with video games.
7. Use of video games to escape or relieve a negative mood (e.g., feelings of helplessness, guilt, anxiety).

Children dealing with an addiction are usually more mentally fragile than others. Video game addicts are no different. Because video game addiction is a very new development in the world of mental health, there are relatively few treatment options available for curing addicts. Most times, cognitive-behavioral therapy (CBT) has been employed as a treatment modality of choice for video game addiction. CBT involves changing the thoughts that contribute to unhealthy gaming habits and also, modifying the behaviors to slowly reduce the amount of time spent playing video games. Aside CBT, other treatment options for video game addiction include:

1. At first, video game addiction books offering self-help treatment for excessive gaming may help. For those who are unable to find a qualified therapist or afford more expensive treatment options, step-by-step guides to stopping video game addiction can be a simple, convenient, and helpful alternative.
2. Perhaps the next and most common strategy for dealing with addiction is in-house therapy involving modification of family systems, interactions, and family dynamics that may be risk factors for gaming addiction. Family therapy is more common when the identified client is a child or teen..
3. One-on-One counseling with a psychologist or therapist who specializes in treating video game addiction.
4. Wilderness therapy involving the complete removal of the individual from environments where video games are accessible. Wilderness therapy has been used as an intervention for a variety of child and adolescent behavioral problems and is starting to be offered for video game addiction as well. Similar to in-patient treatment for video game addiction, wilderness therapy is generally very expensive and may not be offered locally.
5. Video game addiction books offering self-help treatment for excessive gaming. For those who are unable to find a qualified therapist or afford more expensive treatment options, step-by-step guides to stopping video game addiction can be a simple, convenient, and helpful alternative.

Video Games and ADD/ADHD

Attention deficit hyperactivity disorder (ADHD) is one of the most common childhood disorders. There are approximately 6.4 million diagnosed children in the United States according to the Centers for

Disease Control and Prevention [23] This condition is sometimes also called attention deficit disorder (ADD), but this is an older term. The term ADD is used to refer to someone who had trouble focusing, but was not hyperactive.

Video games have been found to have positive effects on children with ADHD [24] Children with this disorder are often unable to concentrate on basic tasks and activities. However, they *are* well-known to have the ability to focus on games. Due to this surge in attention while engaged in video gaming, the learning potential of educational games can often be transferred to children suffering from this disorder by carefully selecting the game and taking the time to plan gaming schedules. Games that require strategic thinking, a working memory, and demand forethought and planning can instill these positive effects in kids.

However, it is not all roses and no dirt. Video games, while having an inherent potential to be an effective tool for imparting knowledge in kids with ADHD, can also have negative effects on kids living with the disorder. An Iowa State University study [25] of some 3,000 children and adolescents from Singapore, measured over 3 years, found that children who spent more time playing video games were more impulsive and had more attention problems. Researchers interpreted the findings to suggest that video game playing can "compound kids' existing attention problems". The research showed that There's no evidence of causality between ADHD and video gaming yet [26].

Since the difficulty to pay attention is widely associated with ADHD, it tends to be the first thing teachers, parents, and clinicians suspect. But there are a number of other possibilities that can be contributing to attention problems. To avoid misdiagnosis, it's important that these other possibilities, which are not always obvious, not be overlooked.

The topic of the relationship between video games and ADD/ADHD is still relatively unexamined by science. A therapeutic use of certain video games is already visible here and there and might start sooner or later for a broader audience.. So, you must endeavor to use your gut feeling in this area. If your kid has the disorder, it is advisable to watch them carefully while they are engaged in video games, ask your professional advisers and limit their screen time as necessary.

EVALUATING YOUR CHILD'S GAMING CONTENT_

THIS CHAPTER FOCUSES on educating parents on how to evaluate their children's gaming content and habits, especially in the context of the before-mentioned good, bad, and ugly content.

How to Evaluate

Let us now turn to helping you understand just how to take control of the situation by evaluating the gaming content and the locations where games are played.

Research work

Before allowing your child to play any game, first of all, take your time to research said game. How do you research a game and determine it is appropriate for your child?

1. Use Official sources

Official sources here refer to the official platforms where games are offered. Examples of these are the mobile app stores – Apple Store, Microsoft Store, Play Store, Playstation Store, Steam for PC games, Mac App store for Macintoshes, and retail outlets (for games on all platforms).

However, the mobile app stores offer greater control over app content than the other aforementioned platforms. These platforms have several regulations which game makers must comply with before their products are accepted for publication on the platform's store. At the moment, the regulations are much stricter in Apple's App Store than in the other app stores. One important hint: There is no control regarding the age group a particular mobile app is published for (see also below)!

Other reasons why the use of official sources is recommended is about the security of the software itself (better security in regards to malicious elements) and the availability of reviews and ratings (see below).

2. Age Limitations

There are so many games in the market, either available for free or for a price. Apart from satisfying other conditions for publication on the platforms mentioned above, further information is provided in the descriptions of games. One piece of important information is the age restriction. Games are expected to carry information indicating what age the games are appropriate for. The age limitation requirement is based on the fact that not all games are appropriate for all ages owing to their contents.

Therefore, it is not surprising that some games, for example, can be rated for persons above the age of 12 while others, for example, can be for adults only, making your work much easier as a parent. You, therefore, should ensure your child is playing a game appropriate for his or her age. However, considering that the developers of most mobile games rate their own games, game ratings might, in some instances, not provide accurate information about what age group particular games are aimed for. Pegi.info is often used in European countries and can be trusted, Entertainment Software Rating Board (ESRB) is another known rating standard mostly used in the USA. Most countries use their own rating systems (e.g. Germany with USK, Japan with Computer Entertainment Rating Organization, the IARC internationally). There are also other programs which rate games, such as the kidSAFE Seal Program. It is important, therefore, to take these type of rating but also the cognizance of user reviews of games into account. Again, these ratings to not yet include mobile games! Mobile games are rated by the developers themselves and therefore cannot be fully trusted. In order to evaluate the appropriateness of mobile games, parents need to check the games by themselves or use reviews (see below).

3. User Reviews

Official sources or platforms where games are offered to people have one wonderful feature built into them: user reviews. Each app has a review page or section on the various stores; it is usually right below the general description of the app or game. Here, users can leave comments about the app or in our case, game. Such comments can relate to technical difficulties, design and even contents. Where you find several users giving the same negative comment about a game, especially if such comment relates to content, there is a very high possibility they are right. In fact, some platforms allow other users to indicate their support for any review by adding a feature called LIKE and DISLIKE. Therefore, instead of having to read through thousands of comments to be able to draw up a general inference, you may also consider the number of likes or dislikes that a review has. As user it is easy to get a feeling whether the game is appropriate for the kid or not. It is also recommended to watch the video- and media content offered as teaser for the games in order to evaluate the games.

Additionally, other online platforms offer even much deeper information and reviews about games. It is just possible that a particular game has been the subject of comprehensive review by gaming experts and enthusiasts on such other platforms. Be sure to check them out, too, as they can reveal a point that is not readily available on the games' official platforms. Good sources are video game magazines, online gaming magazines, and Youtube. Especially Youtube is full of videos containing game reviews of all sort.

Locations of pleasure

Evaluating games back or forth - there is little point in pretending to play games if the child can do what he wants elsewhere. The question of where your child's can play games has been narrowed down to three places: the home, the school and amongst friends. Most games today are played either at home or on the move. Parents should therefore be aware that a time limit on games should also apply to places beyond their home Internet router. Thanks to parental control over data traffic on mobile phones, it is technically possible to restrict at least some games or the usage time in general. Nevertheless, separate rules should apply to school hours or similar. Within the school rules for the use of game devices are necessary. If this is not the case, it would be advisable to encourage them. Despite school digitization and support packages, best practice approaches in dealing with (learning) games are still a long way off. It can therefore be useful to discuss sensible rules with the school. The same applies to the circle of friends. This in particular can have both positive and negative effects on children's playing behavior. Here the parents and teachers should be consulted and the times and/or the games or media consumption used should be discussed with them.

Introduction

Educational games are games designed primarily for educational purposes, but may even only have incidental or secondary educational value. These games are usually structured to assist people in learning certain subjects, reinforce development, understand historical events or cultures, or help them to learn a skill as they play. Certain games have been developed for use in learning across several platforms and devices, and have increased in complexity overtime. Examples of such games can be found in board games, card games, and video games. Over the years, game-based learning has garnered of interest from research, governments, schools and parents the world over.The increasing successes that have been enjoyed by gamed-based learning is largely due to its inherent capacity to join the tiring task of learning and the exhilaration of playing games. Experts have found this combination of playing and learning as the key to developing core abilities and knowledge in people, and especially children. Nevertheless, due to the lag of research, there is still no common agreements or standards in that field which highlights the problematic situation this topic is in today.

With the explosion of technological devices and the rise in consumer demand for learning games [27], there has been a shift in what types of games people play. Video or electronic gaming has become more widely used than traditional board games (at least for the non-educational games). This shift, is also due to the immersive tendencies of video games[28]. Video gaming often requires the player to assume a fictional character, identify with it, and solve deeply engaging virtual problems or challenges

> Educational games are getting more and more popular. Analysts predict global game-based learning industry will hit $17 billion by 2023!

The concept of game-based learning, however established and advantageous, has been met with significant amounts of criticism and skepticism, especially from parents. Because of its close association with electronic games, game-based learning outcomes and the potential to impact positively on children has been questioned, so much that some "experts" have even gone on to make claims that learning by playing is harmful to young people. Some of the benefits of game-based learning already mentioned in the previous chapters include:

1. Engagement and drive. Learners are often motivated by hands-on and active learning opportunities. The students are able to work on accomplishing a goal just by "gaming". They experience the consequences of the actions, which is one of the ways that a game-based learning experience is similar to real life. Educational games are motivating so that the kids do not lose their drive during the learning experience.
2. Improvement in cognition. Children learn to use their strategic thinking skills, including using logic to make sound decisions and to plan ahead by making predictions about what might happen next. Children also develop strong problem-solving skills. They'd need to think quickly and without hesitation, which is a skill that will serve them throughout their lives.

Learners also learn how to think creatively and plan out their moves a few steps ahead. The game-based learning environment results in higher retention rates compared to book learning.

3. Development of basic skills. Games allow kids to practice and develop physical skills such as hand-eye coordination. They can also work on spatial skills and fine motor skills. Interactive games help kids to communicate in integrated learning environments.
4. Rapid feedback. Learners benefit from the quick feedback mechanism in place during game playing. Instead of having to wait days or even weeks for an assignment or test grade, students get instantaneous results about whether or not they made a good decision. They also get to find out the long-term effects of their decision-making. One decision at the beginning of a game could have lasting effects throughout play. The rapid feedback helps kids realize when they made a good decision or a bad one. This motivates to get better.

From basic identification skills to reading, writing, typing, and math skills of all kinds, educational games offer many benefits to players. These games help kids develop cognitive, social, and physical skills simultaneously. Game-based learning improves essential life skills such as cooperation and teamwork.

Promoting Healthy Gaming Habits

The importance of physical activity for humans cannot possibly be overstated. It is even more important to children who, especially in the early stages of their growth and development, require a lot of physical movements to keep in shape and grow optimally. The role of physical activity in the lives of children is even more pronounced today, in the face of the high – and increasing – pediatric obesity rate. Kids spend tremendous amounts of time playing video games, a trend that has encouraged a sedentary lifestyle in them. Since gaming devices are not going away any time soon and we cannot possibly prohibit kids from engaging in them totally, we must tweak certain settings and structures in these games to encourage movements and thus make kids more active.

Movement during Gaming

The importance of physical activity for humans cannot possibly be overstated. It is even more important to children who, especially in the early stages of their growth and development, require a lot of physical movements to keep in shape and grow optimally. The role of physical activity in the lives of children is even more pronounced today, in the face of the high – and increasing – pediatric obesity rate. Kids spend tremendous amounts of time playing video games, a trend that has encouraged a sedentary lifestyle in them. Since gaming devices are not going away any time soon and we cannot possibly prohibit kids from engaging in them totally, we must tweak certain settings and structures in these games to encourage movements and thus make kids more active.

A 2013 report from the Institute of Medicine [29] concluded that children who are more active "show greater attention, have faster cognitive processing speed and perform better on standardized academic tests than children who are less active." And a study released in 2017 by Lund University in Sweden shows that students, especially boys, who had daily physical education, did better in school[30]. John Ratey, an associate professor of psychiatry at Harvard Medical School and the author of "Spark: The Revolutionary New Science of Exercise and the Brain," said: "Movement activates all the brain cells kids are using to learn, it wakes up the brain" [31].The "Let's Move" initiative [32] was initiated helping to bring movement and the health of children into the public consciousness.

Play-based preschools and progressive schools (often with open room plans, mixed-age groups, and an emphasis on creativity and independence) are seeing increased popularity. Enrichment programs engaging children in movement with intention (yoga, meditation, martial arts) are also gaining traction. These kinds of methods seek to give children back some of the agency their young minds and bodies crave. Mindfulness [33] practices such as guided breathing and yoga can help mitigate the core symptoms of ADHD in children, [34] [35] while the arts [36] encourage self-expression and motor-skill development. Electronic gaming can be used as assistance here either by offering reminders to move (like intelligent watches to) or as guide.

Movement is an important part in day-to-day learning life for kids. This is also true for gaming – especially educational gaming. This does not mean that an educational game where kids calculate math tasks have to look like a sports event. A good educational game must be able to teach the subject to a younger kid by using elements of movement and elements of motivation through gamification. The empirical evidence to support the educational effectiveness of electronic games in health education and physical education is still rather limited, but the findings present a positive picture overall [38]

In brief: use games where younger kids can use their entire body as well. In addition, watch out that children also participate in real-world movement activities in school, clubs or just in the yard.

Eating habits during gaming

It is not uncommon for kids to eat and play electronic games simultaneously. Most foods kids enjoy consuming during gaming are junk foods of all types. Despite the generic debates about what is the right food for your kids and the inconclusiveness of the results therein, you must ensure to restrict your kids' consumption of "junk food" such as:

- Sodas, including coke
- Sugary foods and snacks
- Food and drinks high in artificial ingredients such as flavoring or coloring ingredient, especially those that contain none or negligible amounts of nutritional content.
- Snacks roasted in unhealthy oils (industrialized oils like sunflower, canola oil etc.)

While restricting these foods, you must put in place measures that prevent kids from relapsing into their bad eating habits. These measures can be:

- Ensuring that they eat together with the family at the table when necessary (and without distraction by media consumption)
- If snacks during gaming sessions cannot be avoided altogether, then encourage them to stick to veggies, fresh fruits, untreated nuts, water (many kids forget drinking during games), and other healthy foods.

In brief: Limit eating during gaming sessions and encourage healthy eating.

Diseases and disabilities

New technologies enable children with disabilities to experience games in the same way other children can do it – and even together with other children. A team-based game where everyone uses her or his specific possibilities given by the game to progress together is a wonderful aspect of game-based learning.

On the other side, there are certain conditions such as epilepsy, ADD/ADHD, and other brain related issues that might be negatively (possibly also positively) affected by games. As parents and teachers, it is important to consult physicians in this regard and to act responsible based on the expert advice.

In brief: Ask your doctor about game use for children with special conditions.

Electro smog

In 2011, the World Health Organization (WHO) and the International Agency for Research on Cancer (IARC) classified electromagnetic fields as "possibly carcinogenic to humans (Group 2B), based on an increased risk for glioma, a malignant type of brain cancer, associated with wireless phone use"[48]. Most gadgets emit electromagnetic radiation, an energy type that cannot be seen or felt, but whose effects have been observed to be negatively on human cells and tissues. Though the nature of any electro smog effects upon humans remains controversial. Studies in mice have shown that environmental electromagnetic waves tend to suppress the murine immune system with a potency similar to NSAIDs (nonsteroidal anti-inflammatory drugs) [38]

With regards to the environment, the results of ongoing debates about the potential harm of electronic radiation are always a matter of discussion depending on who publishes the most recent study in that field. This also remains during the introduction of 5G-networks. The following generic recommendations are given, as regards children's exposure to electro smog:

- Blue lights coming from LEDs may influence certain functions of the brain. As parents it is important to limit the amount of time kids sit in front of a screen. Most devices today have a blue-light filter – switch it on!

- Other electronic radiation coming from 3G, 4G and 5G-networks, WLAN antennas, Bluetooth signals and so on should be removed from the children's bedrooms as much as possible. Parents should ensure that the Internet router, tablets, and smartphones are in energy- or flight mode or even turned off completely before bedtime. This also includes Internet connected devices (e.g. all IoT-devices), which will grow substantially more popular over the coming years.

In brief: Limit the exposure to artificial blue light (e.g. from LED) and screens in the evening and in the night. Try to decrease the amount of electromagnetic waves coming from all of the devices including IoT-devices, routers, smartphones, tablets, etc.

Dealing with Stress during Gaming

Reducing stress from an overwhelming digital world, including gaming, is another important factor that needs to be considered. Children should be sure to spend time outside, in nature, and away from electronic devices.

If you notice that your child is stressed out as a result of the games they are playing, you should encourage them to carry out some, or all of the following steps. They should:

- Get outside and get away from any electronic stuff! They should leave the game and go take a walk, run, cycle, or just play in a playground or in nature.
- Take breaks frequently from the game in order to get their head in order and avoid being burned out.
- Use electronics to force movement: As mentioned earlier, some games involve real movement (playing tennis, dancing etc.) in

front of the screen using motion tracking. Most games like that are not focusing on learning too much but they might be a good alternative from time to time to get your kids moving. Another alternative is streaming content for exercises like yoga, muscle building, dancing and any other athletic or relaxation training using the body in front of the screen (e.g. just search YouTube).

- Encourage the kids to get enough sleep– 9-12 hours depending on the age is recommended.
- Listen to some calm and soothing music or any other audio (Audio book, podcast etc.) to help relax and refresh the mind.
- Listen to some calm and soothing music or any other audio to help relax and refresh the mind.
- Consider quitting the game. Some games can be frustrating, and may not be suited for your child's personality or age.

In brief: Kids need to learn to calm down after stressful events and parents need to educate and strengthen them in that regard. Depending on your kids, there are many different possibilities to limit stress in the context of consuming media content.

Other healthy uses of technology

"Internet, tell me everything"

Children ask questions for the answers. For thousands of years humans learned through the parent-children-relationship. But the growing trend of devices in our homes that connect to the Internet and allow us to communicate with artificial intelligence and search engines using our voices is growing. Whether an artificial intelligence will educate our kids in the near future cannot be answered today. Nevertheless, this technological developmed makes it easy for children to ask questions even though there are not able to write or read. Smart home devices (such as Amazon's Echo, Apple's Homepod, Google's Google Home) give us new educational possibilities, such as learning vocabularies and more. But, as usual, this also comes with dangers. These dangers include aspects already mentioned before – especially privacy issues.

If children are able to get answers to many of their questions just using their voices, the responsible handling of the Internet becomes even more important. Parents (and teachers in school) need to teach children:

- What is the difference between regular or public information and private information? When can information and certain private information be given away? Information presented on the web has the tendency to be persistent for a long time.
- Answers from the Internet (e.g. Google, Alexa, Siri etc.) are not 100% reliable.

It is important that kids need to learn that the Internet is a "mess" of millions of servers running websites and databases where everyone in the world can write, say, and present almost anything, even if it is wrong. This freedom of opinion is powerful and good, but hard for children to understand. Good analytical skills and the will to do real research is necessary to get valuable information from the Internet (also see chapter 7).

In brief: Teach your children not to believe everything the Internet tells them, and that privacy is important.

Digital minimalism, focus, and watching yourself

The world's offering of media selections is overwhelming. In fact, many adults are very dependent on their devices. Parents need to consider this because their children will imitate what they see, including the use of electronic devices.

As the parent, limit your use of electronic devices when around your kids, otherwise they may soon realize the "importance" of electronic "toys". Show your kids instead that there is no need for electronic devices to play games, to read and write, to have fun, and to learn and teach them that devices are beneficial as tools in certain circumstances.

The expression is sometimes called digital minimalism, which means to drastically limit the use of any electronic devices and media content in certain circumstances (e.g. after 6p.m., when around your children, on weekends etc.). The constant consumption of news feeds from Twitter, Instagram, Facebook, or emails and whatever form of social media should be reduced to prevent dependence from the gadgets and the ongoing trend to look for news every minute. . Limiting the constant use of electronic devices enables concentration, creativity, and the ability to complete mentally demanding tasks.

It is important to teach children that there are times when a book or a blank page of paper and a pen are the only things they need to get things done!

In brief: Be a role model for your kids in regards to dealing with "electronic toys". Teach your kids the importance of concentration and focus.

One word about age

As children grow their brains and bodies develop constantly. Most kids fall into a normal distribution in regards to this development, meaning they fit into the selected "categories" which are used today (1-3 years,4-6 years etc.). But there are exceptions! Some children are able to play a learning game and really benefit from it, while others do not progress at all. As discussed in the previous chapters, parents and teachers always need to consider the individual behavior of their children. This is also true for older children and the beloved topic of shoot-em-up games.

Assuming there would be an educational game that melds shoot-em-up and math (e.g. a more realistic version of Timez Attack – see below), watch your kid how they handle this kind of game – especially the math part of it. Some children can play Fortnite (not an educational game!) after doing homework, stay calm and bring back good grades while others can't. This is sometimes not due to age, but to the personality and capabilities of the child.

A special problem arises in the age between 5 and 8. There are kids who can read with 5, others can barely with 8. There is an astonishing amount of games sold for kids in that group that expects them to fluently read and understand the instruction and story. It is a good idea to use the kids' interest for the game in order to get him or her used to reading. However, it does not make sense if the text overwhelms them.

In brief: Despite the age recommendations – watch your kid!

Now it's your turn: How to Recognize a Good Educational Game

Many different games exist and it is the responsibility of parents and teachers to make the right selection for their children. The following part shows some basic questions that everyone should ask before making a decision.

It is essential, if not crucial, to know that not all games advertised as "educational" really are. Some games might come with a bit of learning and a lot of fun, while others are solely built for entertainment. These kinds of games offer little to nothing in terms of educational potential, but rather they get children sucked deeper into the abyss of nonchalant gaming. In light of this reality, a solid knowledge base about real educational games is vital in harnessing the potential of game-based learning. The game recommendations given here are categorized under subjects or skillsets. Since it is impossible to give an overview of all games, each parent need to be able to make the decision based on his / her own opinion. The following serves as advice:

1. Is the content of the game appropriate for the age of my kid?

The points mentioned in the previous chapter should be checked here - age ratings, user reviews, etc. Playing demo versions or watching the game on YouTube or reading reviews also helps you to assess whether the game is suitable. Another question to consider would be: Is the game appropriate for ADHD, epilepsy, and other conditions your child may have? It can be useful to involve experts (doctors etc.) for this question.

2. What subject does the game teach?

Is the game an educational game that offers information on subjects that interest your child, such as STEM-subjects like math, science, reading, writing, music, and art? There are many games that proclaim to be educational, but aren't. A good example is Minecraft, which is often put into the educational category. Even though the constructing and basic surviving is an interesting aspect (and can be used to teach basic things), Minecraft starts to become educational (in the sense of school subjects) if you force children to add the programming perspective in it (e.g. by using redstone circuits or programming languages to extend it). Otherwise, it belongs in the category creative adventure games.

3. What method is used to teach the subject?

There are educational games, which just focus on the subject itself: like calculating math tasks one after each other. It makes sense to use such games for certain topics where a lot of practice is necessary in order to improve (like math calculations, writing, reading). Adult learning software often uses these types of games, too. Nevertheless, most games like this are too focused on one specific topic for children to have fun. And if there is no fun, the child (and adult) will quickly lose interest, as the benefit of game-based learning only works because of the motivational effects of gamification. If your kid likes jump'n'run-games, it is much better to combine this topic with a school subject – like a hero who is jumping through the world must calculate math tasks in order to progress in the game world. The hero can level up and progress only if certain tasks are solved. It can also be interesting if there is a high score or the possibility to interact with other players so that the result to other kid's scores can be compared. Again, it is the parent's choice to find out what methods their kids prefer.

Using virtual reality or augmented reality is another question falling into this category. Despite the lack of educational content available at the time of this writing, the potential of VR and AR should not be underestimated, and should always be observed.

4. Are there any parental control and statistics?

Sometimes it is nice for parents to see the progress kids make within the subject or topic of the game. Some games also allow to switch on or off certain school topics, change classes, level of difficulties, or enable a time limit. Parental control can be very helpful to evaluate the usefulness of a game.

A good educational game needs to:

1. Offer appropriate content
2. Teach the subject specific to the child's needs
3. Enhance the kid's capabilities by using a correct teaching method that uses motivational aspects with a mixture of intensity between teaching and "gaming fun".
4. Enable parents to see the progress

An example is shown below, evaluating how the game *Magic Land ADD/ADHD* answers the questions posed above:

Magic Land ADD/ADHD

1. The game visually shows no violent content, but enemies need to be conquered by using magic spells. The recommended age is kids from 7 (they must be able to read).
2. The game teaches math, reading, writing, some science topics and languages.
3. It is a 2D-jump'n'run game where the subjects are sprinkled in and only necessary if the player needs to use magic. The player can choose how often magic is used, but it is not possible to beat the game without magic.
4. The game offers different grades of difficulty. Parents can select school topics and see the progress through game points. For a kid of 7 and up which can read, but needs to improve certain school subjects and likes jump'n'run games, this game will be fun and a valuable educational game for smartphones and tablets.

Figure 8.1: Magic Land ADHD

In brief: Use the presented simple questions to select a useful game for your children.

The rare selection of good educational games

It was already discussed that the choice of good educational games is very limited today. Nevertheless, this guide shows the platforms and games recommended for children ordered by age that fulfill at least some elements discussed above. Since there are new games releasing every day, this list is only a selection with which parents can start their dive into the world of educational gaming content.

The following overview serves as an aid for content and age:

- Infants under 3 years should not use any electronic games. Visual and acoustic stimuli can be triggered (animals, animal voices etc. with little or no use of media)
- Kindergarten children (from 3 years) - first logic games,

everyday topics

- Pre-school children / school beginners (5 - 6 years) increasing learning orientation in school subjects
- Primary school children (6 - 10 years) - reading, learning, entertainment, creativity
- Pupils (11 years and older) - increasingly mature in the direction of knowledge acquisition and education in specialist subjects

The GBLS

The games listed in the next few chapters will be awarded with a point score - the Gamed Based Learning Score (GBLS). This is between 1 and 6 (1 being perfect, 6 being the worst) and evaluates the quality of learning games based on the criteria of this book.

Note: Some games are mentioned several times, as they can be used well for several age groups.

EDUCATIONAL GAMING PLATFORMS for Preschoolers

Some recommended educational gaming platforms for preschoolers include the LeapFrog LeapTV, VTech InnoTV, Nintendo 2DS, and Android & iOS devices.

Figure 8.2: The LeapTV console

One of the best consoles for preschool kids has to be the LeapFrog LeapTV. Much like all of LeapFrog's lineup of learning-centered toys, it is educational, but incorporates active video gaming that is easy to play. It's also great for this group of children because of the audio instructions and the controllers are made for little hands. With over 100 educator-approved games and videos, children can interact and play with their favorite characters like *Paw Patrol, Bubble Guppies, Disney's Jake and the Never Land Pirates, Frozen,* and many more. There are three ways to play: body motion, pointer play, and classic control; but they all help young gamers learn through motion, creativity, life skills, mathematics, reading, writing, and science. The LeapFrog LeapTV can be played solo or with someone else, and even auto-adjusts game difficulty to your child's age. Please note: not all games offered for this platform is good for learning.

Figure 9.2: VTech InnoTV

Perfect for petite gamers 3 to 8 years of age, VTech InnoTV is an educational gaming system made for preschoolers, but built with the whole family in mind thanks to its multiplayer capability. It connects to your television and comes with four games in language arts, math, problem-solving, and science. It also has a wireless controller made for tiny hands. The InnoTab cartridges and learning software are also compatible with this gaming system so kids can learn with Mickey Mouse, Dora & Friends, and others. Please note: Not all games offered for this system is good for learning.

Figure 9.3 Nintendo 2DS

Perfect for little hands and long car rides, the Nintendo 2DS is one of the best video game systems for kids on the go (especially when the use of the pencil is supported). It is a colorful handheld device with two bright screens and an interactive stylus pen. This gaming system entertains wherever your child may be, and its rugged, hinge-less design ensures the 2DS can withstand the rough and tumble life of a little gamer. While the screens do not display 3-D imagery like the 3DS variety, the 2DS's brilliant screen is fully capable of playing 3DS games such as *Nikoli's Pencil Puzzle, Pokémon Art Academy, Animal Crossing: New Leaf, Tomodachi Life, Brain Age Concentration Training, and Cooking Mama 5: Bon Appetit!*. It must be mentioned however, that most educational games for kids for the Nintendo 2DS platform should be used after the age of 4. The Wii or Wii U can also be used by children in that age especially because it enhances movement through the use of motion controllers. Nevertheless, the number of games for very young kids are limited.

> For kids around age 4, use the 2DS, vTech, and leapTV with stringent time limits.

Android and iOS devices, such as smartphones and tablets, also host a number of educational games for preschoolers. Most of these games are available on the official iOS and Android app stores. Due to the lack of haptic input possibilities and limited usability, these games are less suitable for younger children. Nevertheless, simple content such as recognizing and naming colors, shapes, animals can be useful for small children for a limited time simply by touching and consuming small educational films. Painting using the pencil is also a nice feature of some tablets.

- **Android & iOS Games**

  Bugs and Numbers
  Age: 4-8
  Platform: iOS
  Subject: math
  Score: 3

Description: Bugs and Numbers is a math game for younger children and offers different mathematical topics such as counting, addition, subtraction, reading the time etc. with nice graphics and sounds. In the image it can be seen that different types of mini games can be played like adding coins.

<u>Math Land: Addition Games for kids</u>

Age: 5+

Platform: iOS/Android

Subject: math

Score: 2

Description: Kids need to conquer a world full of quests and solve math task inbetween. The nice graphics and the music together with the story have a motivating effect.

<u>Star Walk Kids</u>

Age: 5+

Plattform: iOS, Android

Subject: Astronomy

Score: 2

Description: Children can better understand astronomy with this program. The playful treatment of the topic is well suited for younger children to deal with the topics solar system and also star images.

Todo Math

Age: 4+

Platform: iOS/android

Subject: math

Score: 2

Description: Todo Math is a math game designed for kids at various stages of development, as well as those with visual and auditory problems.

Elmo Loves ABCs

Age: 4+

Platform: iOS, Android

Subject: Reading

Score: 4

Description: A game scripted from the popular TV show Sesame Street, Elmo Loves ABCs is designed to introduce preschoolers into the world of spelling.

ABCya Games

Age: 4+

Platform: iOS, Android

Subject: variety of subjects

Score: 2

Description: ABCya is an educational gaming provider that creates games for children at all levels in the genres of racing, typing, and so on.

<u>Reading Eggs learn to read</u>

Age: 3

Platform: iOS

Subject: Reading

Score: 3

Description: Reading Eggs learn to read is a multifaceted game that is designed to help kids learn to read. It has different levels to suit the respective levels of the players.

<u>Khan academy kids (3+)</u>

Age: 3+

Platform: iOS, Android

Subject: Math, Reading, Spelling, Logic

Score: 2-3

Description: Khan Academy is a collection of mobile apps combining subjects like math and reading with creative activities like drawing and storytelling. The image shows a selection of the library available for children.

Sago Mini Doodlecast

Age: 3+

Platform: iOS

Subject: Art and reading

Score: 3

Description: It is an impressive game that lets kids express themselves either verbally or through art.

- **Console games**

Sesame Street: Elmo's Musical Monsterpiece

Age: 3+

Platform: Nintendo

Subject: Music

Score: 3

Description: It is a game that seeks out the musical talent in kids through a series of adventures.

Kinect Sesame Street TV and other sesame street games for Wii and

LeapFrog

Age: 4+

Platform: Xbox 360

Subject: Diverse subjects

Score: 3

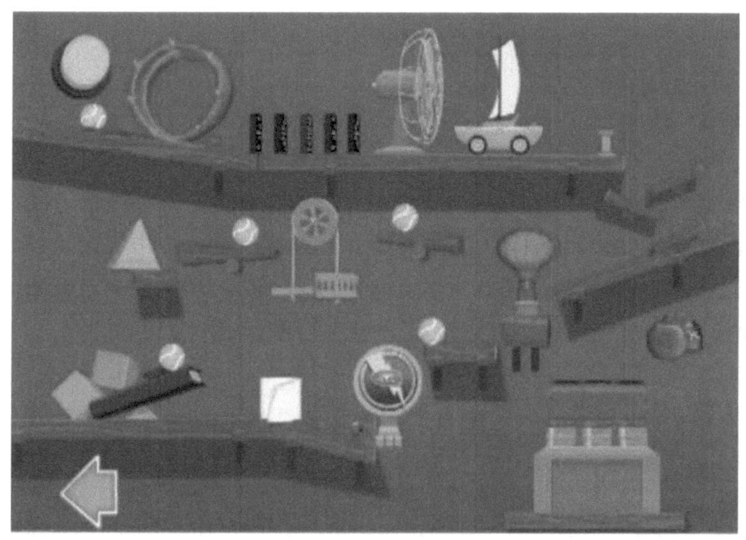

Description: Kinect Sesame Street TV is a game version of the TV show that children have watched for years. In this virtual version, kids can interact with and control characters to perform certain activities. Basic physical interactions is one example children can learn (see figure 9.7).

- **Browser-based games**

  http://www.jumpstart.com/

  Age: 3-13

  Platform: Browser

  Subject: variety of subjects

Score: 3-4

Description: Jumpstart is a platform that creates fun, engaging games aimed at preparing preschoolers for kindergarten.

https://kids.nationalgeographic.com/games/

Age: 3-13

Platform: Browser

Subject: Science

Score: 3-4

Description: kids games produced by (and hosted on) National Geographic are designed to introduce kids to the wildlife in the world. Some of the games offer kids a chance to play with their favorite cartoon characters such as SpongeBob and Ben 10.

- **For little hackers**

https://www.thinkfun.com/learn-coding/

Age: 4+

Platform: Browser

Subject: Coding

Score: No evaluation

Description: Thinkfun is a web-based platform for educational games – such as Robot Turtles and Code Master – designed to introduce children across all ages and levels to the world of programming.

codeSpark Akademie & den Foo

Age: 6+

Plattform: iOS, Android

Subject: Programming / logic

Score: 2

Description: codeSpark enables first logical thinking in the form of programming. The children have to play through levels and improve their skills. Besides, they can develop games themselves.

EDUCATIONAL GAMING PLATFORMS FOR YOUNG KIDS (5-9 YEARS)_

Perhaps the best educational gaming platforms for this age group are the Nintendo 3DS, Wii U, and Nintendo Switch. Nintendo DS and the consoles developed on it are intended for children around the age of 6 years old. The Wii U and Switch series games are also designed for children 6 years or older. Furthermore, the menu guidance when changing games, saving, updating software made by Nintendo (especially the Nintendo DS series) is particularly suited for young children. The Nintendo Switch, however, is a relatively new gaming platform. It is a hybrid device, allowing kids to either dock it with a television and play in HD, or take it with them in a handheld mode. The tabletop mode lets kids play with others, and the handy stand ensures it has a good support. Kids will jump for joy when they play with the included Joy-Con grips that can be used as one, or even two, traditional controllers. Like the Wii, they can detect any up, down, or sideways motion, and are button controlled. With the Nintendo Switch, kids can challenge friends at home, compete with fellow Nintendo Switch users online, or even link up to eight systems together to play wherever they choose. Smartphones and tablets also offer a lot of options in this regard and also offer a wide choice of learning games.

For kids from 5-7 – use Nintendo's 3DS, Wii U, or Switch

- **Android & iOS Games**

Math Evolve: A Fun Math Game

Age: 6-10

Platform: iOS, Kindle

Subject: Math

Score: 3

Description: Math Evolve: A Fun Math Game is a thrilling arcade game that takes kids through basic mathematical concepts including addition, subtraction, multiplication and division. . In order to win, children need to recognize and calculate numbers (see figure 9.8).

SMART Adventures Mission Math – Peril at the Pyramids

Age: 6+

Platform: iOS

Subject: Math

Score: 4

Description: SMART Adventures Mission Math – Peril at the Pyramids is a story-based math game that makes kids solve mathematical problems while on an exhilarating adventure.

CyberChase Shape Quest

Age: 5+

Platform: iOS, Android

Subject: Math

Score: 2

Description: CyberChase Shape Quest is an educational math game that helps kids learn about shapes, geometry, reasoning, and problem solving as they have fun playing.

Magic Land ADHD (7-12)

Age: 7-12

Platform: iOS, Android

Subject: various subjects

Score: 1-2

Description: Magic Land ADHS is a 2D jump'n'run game that teaches mathematics, reading, writing, some science topics and languages. The player has to fight his way through an adventure world and solve tasks with the help of magic. Besides, school topics have to be mastered.

<u>Marble Math Junior</u>

Age: 5+
Platform: iOS, Android
Subject: Math
Score: 2

Description: Marble Math Junior is an excellent game that allows kids to learn to solve math problems while simultaneously engaged in a maze game.

<u>Playful Minds: Math</u>

Age: 5+

Platform: iOS
Subject: Math, Logic
Score: 2

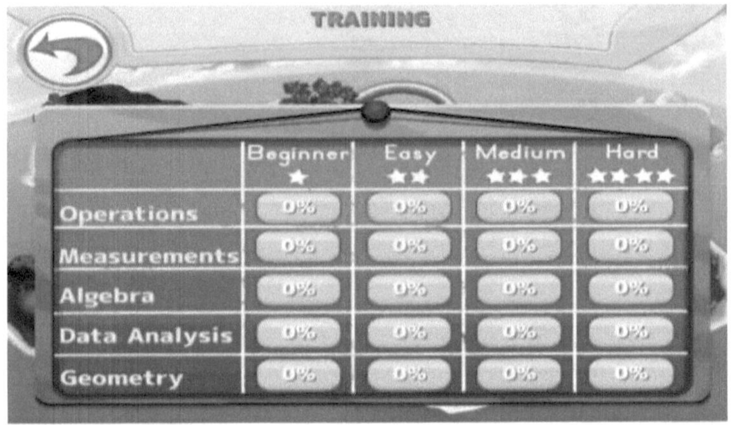

Description: A boy has to conquer a world full of math task in order to solve all quests. Diverse topics as measurements, algebra, geometry etc. are included as shown in the following picture. Statistical elements show the progress of the player.

<u>Sushi Monster</u>

Age: 5+
Platform: iOS
Subject: math
Score: 3

Description: Sushi Monster is a math game through which kids can learn arithmetical concepts like multiplication and addition by feeding monsters. Points are earned for each correct answer, and the monster's anger is increased with each wrong answer.

Crazy Gears

Age: 5+

Platform: iOS

Subject: science

Score: 4

Description: Crazy Gears is an instruction-free games that spurs kids to solve STEM related problems. It enables kids to use their reasoning and problem solving abilities, as it does not come with clues or instructions.

Big Bird's Words

Age: 5+

Platform: Android

Subject: Reading

Score: 2

Description: Big Bird's Words allows kids to learn to pronounce and read things around them by scanning labels, posters, letters, etc. with their device's camera.

Monkey Word School Adventure

Age: 5+

Platform: iOS, Android

Subject: Reading

Score: 3

Description: Monkey Word School Adventure is a game that is specifically designed for young children who are just learning to pronounce words and read.

http://www.mindsnacks.com/

Age: 5+
Platform: iOS
Subject: Reading
Score: 1

Description: Mindsnacks is a learning platform that uses educational games to teach vocabulary, grammar, and some other aspects of the English language and many other languages.

- **Console games**

<u>The Magic School Bus: Oceans</u>
Age: 7+
Platform: Nintendo DS
Subject: Science
Score: 3

Description: The Magic School Bus: Oceans is a story-based game based on the TV series *The Magic School Bus* that teaches kids a lot about aquatic life.

Big Brain Academy

Age: 5+

Platform: Nintendo DS

Subject: math

Score: 2

Description: Big Brain Academy is a game that is designed for kids that are conversant with basic mathematical concepts including addition, multiplication and subtraction, as well as possess financial intelligence.

Disney Art Academy

Age: 5+

Platform: Nintendo

Subject: Art

Score: 3

Description: Disney Art Academy is a game jointly created by Disney and Nintendo to help kids sharpen their artistic talent. It allows kids to draw their favorite Disney characters as well as other characters, persons, or objects they wish to draw.

Professor Layton and His Adventures

Age: 7+

Platform: Nintendo DS, Wii, iOS, Android

Subject: Creative thinking

Score: 3

Description: Professor Layton is a series of adventure games that takes players through the nooks and crannies of London in a quest to unravel mysteries and solve cases.

Brain Age

Age: 7+

Platform: Nintendo DS

Subject: math, reading

Score: 3

Description: Brain Age is a series of games designed for kids across several ages to sharpen their mathematical and memory abilities.

- **PC games**

JumpStart 3D Virtual World

Age: 5+

Platform: Windows

Subject: Math and Reading

Score: 2

Description: JumpStart 3D Virtual World is a science-focused game that rewards kids with "Gems" – currency earned on the game – for completing math and reading challenges.

Reader Rabbit

Age: 5+

Platform: Windows, Mac OS, Nintendo DS

Subject: variety of subjects

Score: 3-4

Description: Reader Rabbit is a series of 8 games developed to help children learn phonics, rhyming, math and ordering.

- **LeapFrog games**

  Cooking Recipes on the Road

  Age: 5+

  Platform: LeapFrog

  Subject: Math

  Score: 3

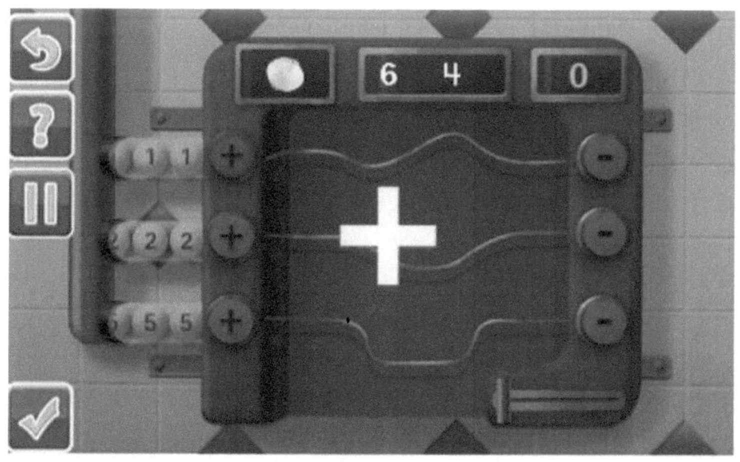

Description: Cooking Recipes on the Road is a LeapFrog game that teaches kids addition, fractions, decimals and temperature, among other concepts, as they serve hungry customers waiting for a snack treat. As it can be seen in the image, children need to make basic calculations using first math skills.

The Magic School Bus: Dinosaurs

Age: 6+

Platform: LeapFrog

Subject: math, science

Score: 3-4

Description: The Magic School Bus: Dinosaurs is an educational game that takes kids back in time to learn about different species of dinosaurs. Kids encounter and solve math problems on their way to the age of dinosaurs.

Super Animal Genius

Age: 5+

Platform: leapfrog

Subject: science

Score: 3-4

Description: Super Animal Genius is a leapfrog game that is developed for the purpose of giving kids information about wild animals.

- **Browser-based games**

https://www.oxfordowl.co.uk

Age: 5-13

Platform: Browser

Subject: Reading

Score: 3-4

Description: Oxford Owl is an online platform that teaches kids to read.

https://www.youtube.com/user/crashcourse

Age: 6+

Platform: Browser

Subject: diverse subjects

Score: 4

Description: Crash Course is a YouTube learning platform that creates educational videos about diverse topics and concepts, which cab help kids increase their knowledgebase.

Geography Now – Youtube channel

Age: 6+

Platform: Browser

Subject: Geography

Score: 4

Description: Geography Now is another YouTube platform that drives kids' education. It gives kids vital knowledge of the world around them, particularly about countries.

- **For little hackers**

  Tynker Junior

  Age: 5+

  Platform: iOS

  Subject: Coding

  Score: 3

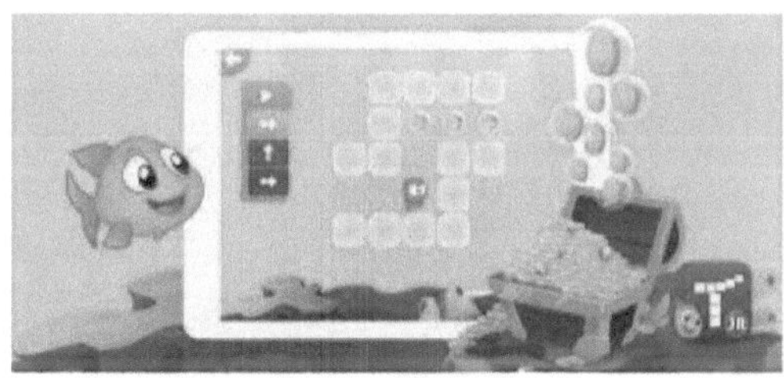

Description: Tynker Junior is a subscription based educational game that introduces kids to coding early on through its three learning areas: Ocean Odyssey, Robots, and Wild Rumble.

Scratch

Age: 5+

Platform: Browser, iOS, Android

Subject: Coding

Score: 2-3

Description: Scratch is a gaming platform that seeks to prepare kids for the life and opportunities of the future by imparting basic knowledge of programming in them.

Sphero

Age 5+

Platform: iOS, Android

Subject: Mechanics, Coding

Description: Using real world building blocks kids can use the Sphero robots (different versions available) to play and learn to interact with robots using their smartphones or tablets.

EDUCATIONAL GAMING PLATFORMS FOR TWEENS (9-12 YEARS)_

THE CHOICE of options is harder for tweens than it is for other age groups. However, it should be mentioned that Nintendo still offers the best options in this regard, followed closely by PC. The PC is somewhat harder to "use" since it requires using a keyboard and a mouse. While some kids are not big fans of the keyboard, others can already type quickly at the age of 10.

Kids in this age range are also likely to admire smartphones and tablets. The choice of games is enormous but good educational games are rare.

Special notes on the use of the smartphone regarding age: This book covers only the use related to educational games and not the use of a smartphone for communication. The age at which children should own a smartphone is discussed worldwide and certainly depends on various aspects that are not covered in this book (e.g. the cultural influence in which children grow up (country, community), or the child's ability to use the device responsibly).

- **Android/iOS games**

  Magic Land ADHD (7-12)

Age: 7-12

Platform: iOS, Android

Subject: various subjects

Score: 1

Description: Magic land ADHD is a 2D jump'n'run game that teaches math, reading, writing, some science topics and languages.

Duolingo

Age: 8+

Platform: iOS, Android

Subject: Languages

Score: 2

Description: With Duolingo the user is able to learn languages based on a concept which uses gamification elements and the use of new technologies like voice recognition. You can also create sentences, learn vocabulary and much more - the improvement process is accompanied by a points system / order motivating.

The Math Space Conqueror Game

Age: 8+

Plattform: Android

Subject: Math

Score: 2

Description: By means of a spaceship you fight your way through space according to the arcade and have to solve tasks. Each step becomes more difficult. The exercises can be adjusted from class 1 to 8.

Math Evolve: A Fun Math Game

Age: 6-10

Platform: iOS, Kindle
Subject: Math
Score: 3
Description: Math Evolve: A Fun Math Game is a thrilling arcade game that takes kids through basic mathematical concepts including addition, subtraction, multiplication and division.

Monster Physics
Age: 10+
Platform: iOS
Subject: Science
Score: 4

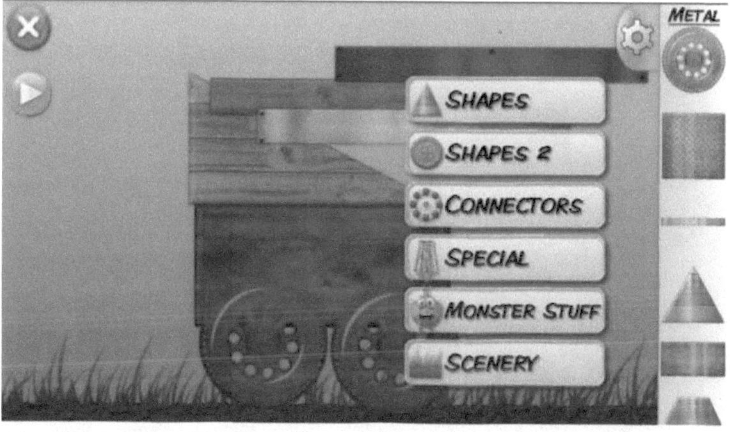

Description: Monster Physics is an exhilarating game that teaches kids physics. Apart from imparting knowledge in kids, the game also allows kids to test their imaginative prowess by building their own devices and instruments. As seen below, different shapes can be placed in order to see physical forces.

Ink Blott Underground

Age: 8+

Platform: iOS

Subject: Reading

Score: 2Description: Ink Blott Underground is a fun, engaging game that teaches kids word formations and usage, by taking them on a thrilling journey underground to eliminate "evil".

Solar Walk™ - Planets System, Orbits, Moons & Size

Age: 7+

Platform: iOS, Android

Subject: Science

Score: 2

Description: Solar Walk™ - Planets System, Orbits, Moons & Size is a game-based learning app that allows kids to learn about the solar system.

In the app, kids can zoom from one cosmic body to the next to discover facts or view a gallery of photos.

Professor Astro Cat's Solar System

Age: 7+

Platform: iOS, Android

Subject: Science

Score: 2

Description: Professor Astro Cat's Solar System is another exciting game-based educational app that imparts knowledge of the solar system in kids. Kids can play trivia games while exploring the solar system, as well as build themselves a rocket ship.

Tower Math

Age: 7+

Platform: iOS, Android

Subject: math

Score: 1

Description: Tower Math is a fun math game that allows kids to utilize and develop their addition, subtraction, division and multiplication skills, while building towers and turning scary monsters to mere numbers.

Flowkey

Age: 7+

Platform: iOS, Android

Subject: Music

Score: 1

Description: Flowkey is an interactive app that teaches players how to play the piano, while receiving instant feedback.

Yousician Guitare

Age: 7+

Platform: iOS, Android

Subject: Music

Score: 1

Description: Yousician Guitare is a fun, subscription-based app that teaches players how to play musical instruments including the guitar, piano, and bass.

- **Browser-based games**

https://www.oxfordowl.co.uk

Age: 5-13

Platform: Browser

Subject: Reading

Score: 3-4

Description: Oxford Owl is an online platform that teaches kids to read.

Legends of Learning

Age: 7+

Platform: Browser

Subject: Science

Score: 3-4

Description: Through more than 1000 curriculum aligned games, Legends of Learning helps bolster kids' knack for scientific reasoning, as well as their knowledgebase.

- **Console games**

  The Magic School Bus: Oceans

  Age: 7+

  Platform: Nintendo DS

  Subject: Science

  Score: 3

  Description: The Magic School Bus: Oceans is a story-based game based on the TV series The Magic School Bus that teaches kids a lot about aquatic life.

Letter Quest Remastered

Age: 7+

Platform: Multiple platforms

Subject: Reading

Score: 2

Description: Letter Quest Remastered is a role playing game that offers kids the opportunity to fight monsters and earn valuable gems by spelling words. In the image it can be seen that children need to spell words in order to progress within the game which is put into a ghostly story.

Professor Layton and his adventures

Age: 7+
Platform: Nintendo DS, Wii, iOS, Android
Subject: Creative thinking
Score: 3

Description: Professor Layton is a series of adventure games that takes players through the nooks and crannies of the famous city of London, in a quest to unravel mysteries and solve cases. Different games were realized on different platforms. The images shows a version on the Nintendo DS.

- **PC games**

Cell Command

Age: 11+

Platform: Windows, Mac OS, Linux

Subject: Science

Score: 2

Description: Cell Command is a science-based game that teaches the ins and outs of how human cells work by engaging kids in mini games.

Kerbal Space Program

Age: 8+

Platform: Windows, Mac OS, Linux, PlayStation

Subject: Science and technology

Score: 4

Description: Kerbal Space Program is a non-violent educational game that makes kids utilize their creative thinking skills to build rocket ships and fly them.

BigBrainz Timez Attack

Age: 7+

Platform: PC

Subject: math

Score: 2

Description: Imagine Learning is a platform that employs engaging 3D gameplay in teaching kids math fundamentals – addition, subtraction, division, and multiplication.

Wildlife Park series

Age: 8+

Platform: Windows

Subject: Science

Score: 4

Description: Wildlife Park is a construction game released in 2003. Like Zoo Tycoon and Zoo Empire, the game engages players in building a wildlife park or zoo.

Apollo 11 VR

Age: 10+

Platform: PC-based VR platforms

Subject: Space technology

Score: 1

Description: Apollo 11 VR is a game based on one of the greatest journeys ever embarked upon by mankind, the Apollo 11 mission. Through this game, players are offered a firsthand virtual experience of that historic voyage.

Epistory – Typing Chronicles

Age: 8+

Platform: Windows, Mac OS

Subject: Typing

Score: 1

Description: Epistory – Typing Chronicles is a colorful adventure game in which progress is made when words are typed on the screen by the player.

- **For little hackers**

Codespells

Age: 10+

Platform: Windows

Subject: Coding

Score: 1

Description: Codespells is created for players who already have a fundamental knowledge of programming. This can make it frustrating, especially for novices. However, with the right guidance and perseverance, the game soon becomes fascinating to play.

<u>Tynker</u>

Age: 8+

Platform: Browser

Subject: Coding

Score: 2

Description: Tynker is a browser-based, visually impressive platform that teaches kids the fundamentals of programming. It contains paid programming courses that kids can be enrolled on, as well as free coding games.

<u>Hopscotch</u>

Age: 8+
Platform: iOS
Subject: Coding
Score: 2

Description: Hopscotch is a platform that teaches kids coding skills using cool, drag and drop, interactive interfaces. Though Hopscotch is free to use, payment of a certain monthly stipend unlocks premium features such as liberty to add own pictures and customize personal profiles.

<u>Roboter BQ Zowi</u>

Age: 5+
Platform: iOS, Android
Subject: Building, Mechanics
Score: 2-3

Description: Cargo-Bot teaches kids programming through the use of an interactive robot. The kids need to understand how the robot is build using mechanical and electronical elements. Then they can play with the robot by programming it using an app.

OSMO Genius Kit / Osmo Coding Awbie

Age: 6+
Platform: iOS, Android
Subject: Building, Mechanics
Score: 2
Description: OSMO Genius Kit and the extension of it can be used to start getting programming experience and logical thinking. The advantage especially for younger kids is the use of real building blocks to do that – together with the virtual world of the app.

Cargo-Bot

Age: 10+
Platform: iOS, Android
Subject: Coding
Score: 2
Description: Cargo-Bot is a coding platform that teaches kids programming through the use of an interactive robot that the kid uses to move objects from one point to another during the course of the game.

Codeakid.com

Age: 7+
Platform: Web browser based
Subject: Coding
Score: 3

Description: Codeakid is an online academy to teach kids how to develop programming skills which can be used to change Minecraft using mods or develop generic games / apps.

Lego Mindstorms Fix the Factory

Age: 10+

Platform: iOS

Subject: Coding

Score: 2

Description: Lego Mindstorms Fix the Factory is a programming puzzle game that requires kids to direct a robot to perform certain tasks.

EDUCATIONAL GAMING PLATFORMS FOR TEENAGERS (12 AND UP)_

THE BEST EDUCATIONAL gaming platforms for teens are PCs, tablets and smartphones. The PC offers a vital advantage: kids might start to use it for other purposes as well – like writing and doing homework, typing on the keyboard, programming etc., which are aspects all teenagers should delve into before they leave high school. Similar things can be learned using smartphones or tablets. For learning, smartphone and tablet apps might have some advantages since they offer many interesting features that most PCs do not, such as touch input, speech input, use of digital pens, AR-support, and more. However, there are more educational gaming apps available for smartphones and tablets than for the PC (though web-based games can be run on either platform). It is advised to take time to select the right games through the guiding steps mentioned in this book and by doing research.

Teenagers should stick to tablets, smartphones, & PC.

- **PC games**

SpaceChem
Age: 14+
Platform: Windows, Mac OS, Linux
Subject: Science

Score: 4

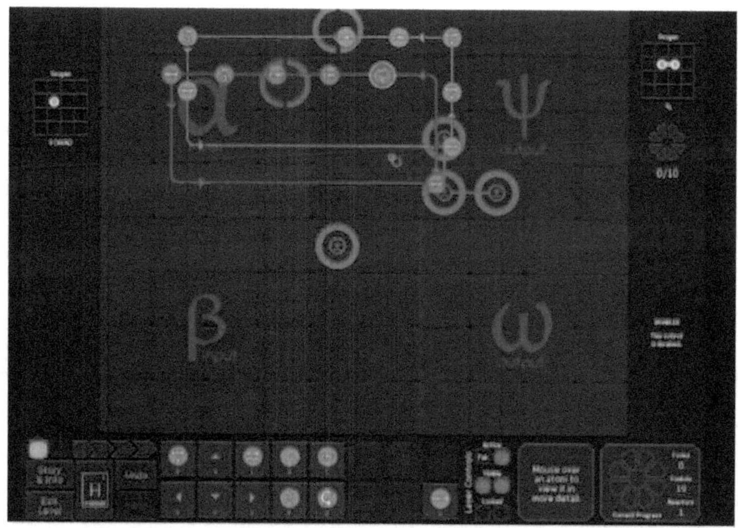

Description: SpaceChem is a game that drives players to use logical reasoning and scientific bases to develop core STEM skills. Because of the complexity of the game, younger players usually require adult guidance to make progress in it. In the image it can be seen that the player need to combine atoms in the right order to create a reaction.

<u>Complete Anatomy</u>

Age: 14+

Platform: Windows

Subject: science

Score: 3

Description: While not really a game, Complete Anatomy uses similar interactivity that games utilize in transferring knowledge from the platform to the player.

Influent

Age: 14+

Platform: Windows

Subject: Language

Score: 3

Description: Influent is a language learning video game designed to motivate people to learn a new language by making vocabulary acquisition and proper pronunciation a fun and rewarding experience.

- **For little hackers**

MAKERbuino

Age: 11+ years

Platform: -

Topic: Physics, Electronics, Programming

Rating: 2

Description: Children who want to build a game console themselves are well advised to use this kit. Developing games for the device is also a challenge afterwards. Parents should support the topics, as they sometimes have a high degree of difficulty.

Arduboy - https://arduboy.com/

Age: 12+

Platform: Arduino

Subject: Coding

Score: 2

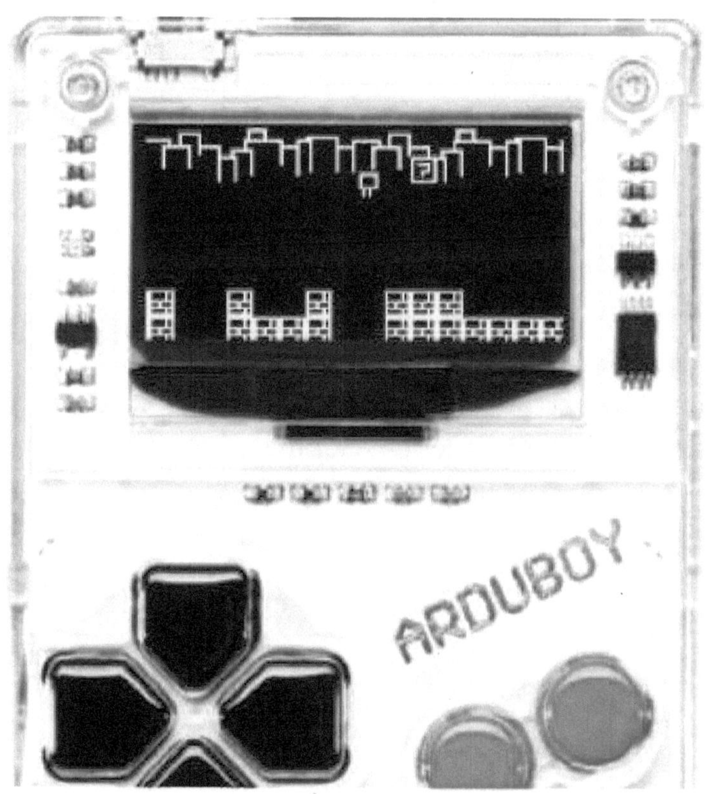

Description: Arduboy is a small and compact gaming platform that hosts an 8-bit game. It is open source, which means, people can modify the pre-installed game or develop and play their own games. In the image a game running on an Arduboy is shown.

<u>Shenzhen I/O</u>

Age: 12+
Platform: Windows, Mac OS, Linux
Subject: Coding
Score: 3

Description: Shenzhen I/O is a puzzler video game allows a player to assume the character of an electronics engineer, to develop products (such as creating circuits and developing programs to run them) for clients.

THE LITTLE HACKER: LEARNING PROGRAMMING SKILLS FOR THE FUTURE_

THE WORLD IS CHANGING RAPIDLY, but predictably. As the industrial age comes to an end, the information technology age will take over (it already has in some parts of the world) and explode rapidly. We are growing to adapt to the demands of this new world – fulfilling most daily tasks with computerized gadgets and procedures. One of the measures we are employing in order to measure up to the technological demands of the modern world is keeping computers of all kinds (smartphones, PCs, etc.) handy, and learning to use them efficiently.

As the world shifts its focus from manual to computerized labor, so must you. And more importantly, so must your children. You must prepare your kids for the jobs and opportunities of the future by engaging them in technology based activities and training early on. A recent Bureau of Labor Statistics report [48] says "software development skills continue to be the most in-demand" STEM (science, technology, engineering, and math) related jobs in the United States, and the White House projects that there will be over one million unfilled jobs in STEM related fields by 2020 [49] It is safe to assume that technology is the future and it is useful to prepare and educate kids in these topics.

Today's kids are different from kids of past generations in many ways, but perhaps one of the most outstanding advantages of the modern kid is their ability to work with technological gadgets. It's not a daunting task to imbibe a tech mindset in your child in an attempt to prepare them for tomorrow's opportunities. Born in the age of Internet and hyper-connectivity, today's kids are digital natives with an ability to pick up and master new technologies with a speed and fluency that boggles the mind. With the right strategies, devices and environment, children learn to work with technological instruments very quickly. If your kid has a knack for opening up gadgets or simply enjoys being around computers, you must encourage, support, and even enhance that interest. Two common ways of enhancing your child's passion for technology are through programming lessons and electronic toys.

Perhaps of the best ways to develop your kid's interest in technology is by encouraging them to learn the language of technology: programming and the understanding of electronics [50]. Computer programming teaches kids skills that are instantly relevant on the job market, and due to the fact that we live in the ever-evolving age of digital transformation, these skills can be employed in various industries. According to the report [51] about STEM occupations issued by the U.S. Bureau of Labor Statistics, the future is incredibly bright for developers, programmers, software engineers, and computer scientists. Job opportunities in computer occupations are forecasted to grow by 12.5% between 2014 and 2024, which will result in more than five hundred thousand new jobs in the field. The economic side is also favorable: 93% of STEM occupations have wages above the national average [50] This means your kids will have amazing chance of excelling in this career and enjoy great financial stability.

There are many educational games out there that teach programming. These games offer coding lessons to kids across various ages and levels of development. Some of these are mentioned in the previous section of this book ("for little hackers").

Electronic toys and kits are specifically designed to teach kids hacking and basic programming skills, and they cater to a range of ages and skill levels. "It's important that we create learning experiences for kids that help to see what's possible for them, what they can do, who they can be, and the changes that they can make to what's around them," said Eric Rosenbaum, who is an electronics kit designer and has a PhD from MIT's Lifelong Kindergarten group [52] There are a number of these toys in the market, which through parents' guidance, can be put to great use by kids. Some of the standout ones include:

- Kano
- LittleBits Gizmos and Gadgets Kit
- SparkFun Inventor's Kit
- DiverseLego-Kits
- Robo Wunderkid Starter Kit
- Mand Labs Kit
- Piper Computer Kit
- Other kits for Raspberry Pi or Arduino

Kano is a simple kit designed for young builders as young as 6. It comes with an instruction manual that contains text and easy to understand diagrams about how to fit the pieces together and make them work.

LittleBits Gizmos and Gadgets Kit is an extremely simple electronic kit that enables kids to learn the basics of circuitry. The simple steps to follow are printed in front of the pack, and the kit looks and feels surreal to kids.

SparkFun Inventor's Kit is designed for relatively older kids, about 10 or older, who have a deep passion for programming and electronics. It is an astoundingly complete and well-organized kit for those trying to learn computer programming and electronics basics.

Lego lovers are not left out of the electronic kits options bag (Lego Mindstorms, Lego Dash Robot etc.). Lego kits are fun and exhilarating to work on,. With Lego kits, kids will learn how software powers hardware, as well as a number of keystone concepts to build on as they continue in their journey to technological literacy.

Robo Wunderkid Starter Kit gives young robotics enthusiasts to build their own bots, as well as operate them. To do this, the kit allows kids to use two apps: Robo Code, to set the bot's behaviors; and Robo Play, which lets kids remotely control their bot.

Mand Labs kit, designed for kids age 6 and above, is a big cardboard box that contains literally everything a kid needs to learn the basics of electronics and circuitry. It also comes with step-by-step instructions for about 50 maker projects that start simple and increase in complexity, as well as 9 hours of video instruction.

Piper Computer kit is made for older kids, or kids who are already conversant with the basic concepts of electronics. It comes with Raspberry Pi unit, a laser-cut wood case, a (small) screen, a battery, and a (very small) mouse, which kids can use to develop their own small computer. Once they've successfully developed their computer, kids can use it to carry out tasks such as playing simple games, typing, and even Internet browsing.

Kits for Arduino-based or Raspberry Pi are now available in abundance. Children from 10 years can let off steam here.

In addition, game engines and construction kits for game development, which partly require programming, should be mentioned once again. Children can give free rein to their creativity and can engage in programming as well as music, sound, graphics and animations with:

Game Maker, Construct, Game Salad, RPG Maker, Mario Maker, Unity 3D, Unreal Engine etc.

Kids are usually glued to their phones and computers for long periods of time texting, playing games, or browsing the Internet. However, some kids show an interest in more than just the basic tasks of electronic gadgets. They want to know how these gadgets work and "think". Such an interest must be taken strongly and encouraged by parents, as it may be an important starting point for the child's journey to technological supremacy. The age of technology is upon us, and the demand for technology-based skills are increasing. This trend is forecasted to surge further into the future, hence, parents must begin today to imbibe the technological mindset in their kids, as well as strengthen their kids' affinities for tech gadgets.

THE POWER OF MOTIVATION: GAMIFICATION STRATEGIES_

GAMIFICATION OF LEARNING is an approach to motivate students to learn by using video game design, principles, and game elements in educational settings in an endeavor to optimize engagement and enjoyment through capturing the interest of the students. Simply put, Gamification is the inculcation of gaming elements into real-life learning situations and is discussed controversially in scientific research[41] [40] .

Games are known to increase motivation in educational settings. The traditional methods and pathways of teaching in the formal education setting, though effective, are not perfect. This fact is evident in the staggering number of students who fail to graduate within the minimum stipulated period of learning. In the U.S., for instance, approximately 1.2 million students fail to graduate each year [42] At the college level, a Harvard Graduate School of Education study "Pathways to Prosperity" reports that just 56% of students complete four-year degrees within six years [43] It's argued that this is due to current systemic flaws in the way we teach. Schools are behind the times. Gamification can assist to motivate. Below are some of the benefits of gamification:

1. It offers a better learning experience. A good gamification strategy with high levels of engagement will lead to an increase in recall and retention.

2. It provides instant feedback so that learners know what they are doing correctly and what they should strive to learn.

3. .Gamification can be applied to diverse fields of learning [44]

4. It gives learners the freedom to fail and try again without negative repercussions [45]

5. It serves as an effective motivator for people with low levels of motivation to learn.It creates chances to increase fun and joy within the classroom [46]

How to Inculcate Gamification into Education

Instructors have tested the theory of gamification and seen positive results [42] There are a number of ways to introduce your classroom to the gamification of education and we're providing you with just a few ideas.

1. In grading

One way of achieving gamification is by abandoning the traditional grading system and adopting the experience points system instead. In this method, students' letter grades are determined by the amount of points they have accumulated at the end of the course, in other words, by how much they have accomplished. One success story is Lee Sheldon, a professor at Indiana University, who gamified his course using this method [42] Because of the extracurricular interests of the current college-age generation (games!), Professor Sheldon attributes success to the fact that "the elements of the class are couched in terms they understand." Students are progressing towards levels of mastery, as one does in games. Each assignment and each test feels rewarding, rather than disheartening. Using experience points allows educators to align levels with skills and highlight the inherent value of education.

2. Awarding students with badges

In this method, students are awarded with badges upon completion of tasks or assignments. This method has worked for the web platform, Khan Academy. As students watch instructional videos and complete problem sets, Khan Academy awards them with points and badges to track progress and encourage perseverance.

3. Integrating educational videos into the curriculum

As earlier noted, gamification allows students to fail and try again without bitter consequences. Students are given a sense of liberty and responsibility—in games, they control the choices they make, and the more agency students have, the better students do. Instant feedback and rewards are external motivators that work. A case study is that of a Mr. Pai, a 3rd grade teacher who was on a mission to make learning fun [42] He disrupted the traditional classroom setting by introducing the Nintendo DS, among other technological devices, into his daily curriculum. Students practiced certain school subjects through the use of computer and video games. In just about 18 weeks, his class went from a below 3rd grade level to a mid-fourth-grade level.

4. Adding a bit of competition

Competition is a means of getting people, especially children, to work harder towards a particular goal or a certain task. The fear of failure and ecstasy of victory are motivating factors that push children to pit their best in competitions. After all, everybody wants to be on the leaderboard.

We have seen gamification in practice in a variety of settings: completing a punch card to win a free sandwich, receiving a badge for being the first of friends to check in at a particular restaurant, or expanding our profiles on LinkedIn to bring the "completion bar" up to 100%. Gamification has even worked its way into the automotive industry with the innovative dashboard of the Ford Fusion hybrid. A high-resolution display features a rendering of vine-like leaves. Waste gas, and your vines wither. Conserve, and they blossom. Gamification remains a viable and promising pathway to increase high levels of motivation in learners, and hence, improved assimilation and retention rates.

What is missing in the World of Educational Gaming?

Not a lot has been done in the area of game-based learning. There are many educational games that teach solid subjects and concepts but miss real innovative approaches. The world needs educational games that:

- Teach a relevant subject for the target group (kids in this case).
- Use the right mixture of "learning" and "gaming". The learning part has to be subliminal enough that the gaming experience is not disturbed but intensively enough that the subject is taught.
- Uses gamification to create constant motivation and challenges might also include social interaction with others.
- Offer multiple features available on the chosen platform. Instead of just transferring paper-based math worksheet on screen, the use of AR/VR, camera, GPS, Gyroscope, Accelerometer, Magnetometer, online-connection must continue to be offered in new technology.
- Do not overload the target group with content or features.
- The level of difficulty can be customized parents retain control over the content.
- Offer statistics to parents so they can their child's progress, strengths, and weaknesses.

Considering the amount of games available in a constantly growing industry, it is unbelievable that educational games with a GBLS of 1 and 2 are so rare. If the GBLS score is broken down into the different platforms on which games can be played on, it is even more disappointing.

For PlayStation and Xbox there are almost no really good educational games.

Good educational games on PC are growing more and more scarce every year. The potential of VR is not used enough in this market.

There are good offers, which require a web browser and are best used with a PC or Mac, though.

Despite the many choices for Nintendo consoles, most educational games are either for the Nintendo 2/3DS or the older Wii, but not for the newest console Switch (yet).

The gigantic choice in educational games in the mobile market makes the smartphone and tablets as the top platform for educational content but the quality is extremely volatile despite the big potential. Augmented reality might be a new feature, which can be used in educational learning experiences in the near future.

The question is – what are the reasons why the choices are so limited?

It seems that there is more money to make realistic games than educational ones. The average age range of people in 2017 who play games at most are people between 21-35 years old, closely followed by the 36-50 year olds [[39]

Even though the educational landscape in schools is starting to switch to the use of electronic-based equipment, the use of game based learning is still limited. Pedagogical decisions are based on scientifically proven theses and these barely exist. Educational concepts develop over a longer period of time than the market of electronics. This is why schools will always lag behind and why it is important that parents and teachers go ahead and experiment responsibly by themselves.

TYING THE KNOT: GETTING IT ALL TOGETHER_

What You Have Learned

This book has offered a comprehensive outlook on the world of gaming in general and educational gaming in particular. Here are the main takeaways from each of the chapters of this book:

Chapter 1:

• Parenting is a tasking, intriguing, and ultimately rewarding job. Children, especially when very little, need the guidance and leadership of adults for optimum overall development. Parents, therefore, need to step up to this responsibility and take charge of their kids' growth and development.

• Technology has massively affected the way kids experience the world and behave. Tech gadgets have practically become extra limbs on our bodies, and particularly for children. We depend largely on technology to carry out myriads of tasks. This makes it all the more important to learn how to handle them responsibly at an early stage.

• Children are spending massive amounts of time indoors and the obesity rate has risen to the skies in the last few decades. Scientists have attributed that to the sedentary lifestyle led by most youngsters today. Kids need to move more!

Chapter 2:

• Seeing from the perspective of complexity of the world, modern parents have more parental duties than those of past generations. Since the explosion of technology, tech gadgets have literally taken over the lives of their children, as most now own smartphones and computers. While these gadgets can be used to beneficial ends, they can also pose dangers to the health of children. The modern parent as well as the teacher is, therefore, saddled with the responsibility of ensuring optimum usage of these gadgets.

• There is no shortcut to good parenting. It takes a lot of hard work and commitment. Parenting is a duty that is very often neglected or, at best, mishandled.Only through meticulous planning and execution of parental responsibilities can one achieve their parenting ambitions.

• Children are engaging less with personal computers and more with smartphones. The ease of operating smartphones has made them appealing to people, especially children, as the preferred device for computational and entertainment purposes. Parents serve as role models in this respect.

• Smartphones and tablets are now the most popular gaming platforms, superseding PCs and game consoles. This is mostly due to the copious supply of the former, relative to the latter. This is not true for good educational games though.

• Modern gadgets offer myriads of possibilities and advantages, but they do come with almost as many risks and dangers. Parents and teachers need to educate kids in that matter.

Chapter 3:

• The emergence of the Internet has opened up pathways to easier and more effective methods of carrying out routine activities. The Internet has made peer-to-peer communications easier through the introduction of social media and emailing. This opens possibilities and threats, which kids need to be educated in.

• Online-based games – analogue or digital used - are a way for kids to interact and socialize on the Internet, as well as a tool for effecting malicious attacks on unsuspecting children. Here, too, important rules of conduct apply that children must learn.

Chapter 4:

• Games are an effective way to teach kids about topics that would otherwise be incomprehensible and difficult for them to understand. The quality of attention that children pay to gaming can be used to impart knowledge in them.

• Game-based learning has the potential to affect the intellectual capacity of children positively. Cognitive, intellectual, and social strengths are some of the vital capacities a child can gain from their use of educational gaming content.

• Skillsets learned and applied in educational games can often be applied in solving real-life problems. Certain educational games teach complex concepts that enhance problem-solving prowess in children. These skills can then be utilized to maximum effectiveness in solving real-world problems.

Chapter 5:

• Parents should encourage their children to play good educational games because they have the potential to explain complex subjects in fun and engaging ways. They can also lead to improvements in children's educational performance.

• There are lots of reasons why parents should encourage their kids to play educational games. Some of these reasons are improvement in social interaction, the ability to form connections and networks, and improvement in players' intellectual capacity.

Chapter 6:

- Kids often need the guidance of older people in their gaming journey. They need people to explain what they are interacting with to them, and ensure that they engage with gaming content appropriately.
- Parents are advised to participate in electronic games with their kids – especially the younger ones. By engaging in these games with them, you are able to have a firsthand knowledge of the gaming content they are exposed to, rate, make judgments concerning the content, and monitor your kid's usage of the content.
- Parents can restrict children's gaming time and content by putting certain measures in place. These include electronic, Internet, and physical restrictions by using schedules, monitoring activities, and filters.
- Video games, if utilized correctly, can benefit children with ADD/ADHD. While some scientific studies have highlighted the positive effects of video games on children with ADHD, some have shone light on their negative effects. Whatever the case, it is important that parents know their children and what works for them.

Chapter 7:

- Parents can monitor, to a great extent, the content of games their kids are exposed to. They can use a number of methods to keep a close watch on their kids' gaming activity and content. Some of these measures include use of official resources on games, reading user reviews, and employing age restrictions highlighted on most games.

Chapter 8:

- Educational games are developed with the purpose of imparting real-world knowledge in kids. However, due to the lack of a standard for learning games, the quality of learning games differs considerably.

• Different gaming platforms and devices are suited to different age ranges and educational levels. Nintendo arguably provides the best gaming platforms for kids between 4 and 12 years, through their Wii / Wii U, DS and Switch devices which also includes the choice of educational games. For older kids, personal computers, smartphones and tablets offer better educational gaming content.

Chapters 9-12:

• Educational games are categorized according to ages of players, as well as their educational levels. However, parents should pay more attention to the development and performance of their own child.

Chapter 13:

• While most kids spend time using modern gadgets only for gaming and Internet purposes, some kids have a keen interest in acquiring a deeper understanding of these gadgets. Kids that show early interest should be encouraged to go into building kits, electronics, programming or other STEM-based career paths, as these have been forecasted to create the majority of jobs in the near future.

Chapter 14:

• The concept of gamification can been employed by many educators and instructors alike to increase motivation during the learning process.

• Gamification employs fun, exciting ways to present educational content to students in a manner that they love and enjoy. Through the gamification of education, students can be motivated to learn and improve.

CONCLUSIONS_

Game-based learning offers a different strategy than the traditional classroom learning process. Through leaps in technology, games have been used as a medium to offer both entertainment and training simultaneously. The effects of this combination have been found to be astounding in the mental, emotional, intellectual and physical development of people and especially children. However, since most games in the modern era are offered through electronic media, they cannot be exempt from the hazardous effects of those medias. Caution must be taken, therefore, to guard children against the harmful effects of games. Parents are urged to tightly hold onto the knowledge they might have gained from this book and to try to apply it so their kids get optimum results from educational games which are appropriate in this modern world. The media world, which also includes computer games, has become part of the culture and thus an important part of the development of most children. Accordingly, this issue should be dealt with by schools and parents.

1. Wartella, E., Rideout, V., Lauricella, A., & Connell, S. (2013). *"Parenting in the Age of Digital Technology: A National Survey"*. Report of the Center of Media and Human Development, School of Communication, Northwestern University.

2. A Common Sense Research Study (2013). *"Zero to Eight: Children's Media Use in America 2013"*, https://www.commonsensemedia.org/file/zero-to-eight-2013pdf-0/download, accessed August 2018

3. Lenhart, A. (2015). *Teens, Social Media & Technology Overview 2015.* Pew Research Center, http://www.pewinternet.org/2015/04/09/teens-social-media-technology-2015/, accessed August 2018

4. Lenhart, A. (2015). *"A Majority of American Teens Report Access to a Computer, Game Console, Smartphone and a Tablet"*, http://www.pewinternet.org/2015/04/09/a-majority-of-american-teens-report-access-to-a-computer-game-console-smartphone-and-a-tablet/, accessed August 2018

5. American Families See Tablets as Playmate, Teacher and Babysitter (2012), , https://www.nielson.com/us/en/insights/new/2012/america-families-see-tablets-as-playmate-teacher-and-babysitter.html, accessed July 2018

6. Alghamdi, Y. (2016). *"Negative Effects of Technology on Children of Today"*. Pakland University.

7. Journal of Child Obesity, http://www.imedpub.com/scholarly/childhood-obesity-statistics-journals-articles-ppts-list.php, accessed June 2018

8. Arthur, C. (2012). Dell Revenues Slump as Tablets and Smartphones Eat into Market. The Guardian.

9. Ybarra, Michele & Mitchell, Kimberly. (2005). *"Exposure to Internet Pornography among Children and Adolescents: A National Survey"*. Cyberpsychology & behavior : the impact of the Internet, multimedia and virtual reality on behavior and society. 8. 473-86. 10.1089/cpb.2005.8.473.

10. Gee, J. P. (2003). "What video games have to teach us about learning and literacy". New York, NY: Palgrave Macmillan.

11. Squire, K. (2004). *"Replaying history: Learning world history through playing Civilization III". (*Unpublished doctoral dissertation). Indiana University Bloomington, USA.

12. Siegler, R. S., & Ramani, G. B. (2008). *„Playing linear numerical board games promotes low-income children's numerical development"*. Developmental Science, 11(5), 655-661.

13. Liu, E. Z. F., & Chen, P. K. (2013). *„The Effect of Game-Based Learning on Students' Learning Performance in Science Learning – A Case of "Conveyance Go""* Procedia - Social and Behavioral Sciences 103 (2013) 1044 – 1051

14. Milczynski, K.A., (2010). *"Literature Review: Effectiveness Of Gaming in the Classroom"*. Michigan State University.

15. Mayer, R.E., (2016). *"What Should Be the Role of Computer Games in Education?"* SAGE Journals. Vol 3, Issue 1, 2016. https://doi.org/10.1177%2F2372732215621311

16. Griffiths M. (2005). *"Video games and health"*. BMJ (Clinical research ed.), 331(7509), 122-3.

17. Marc Palaus, Elena M. Marron, Raquel Viejo-Sobera, Diego Redolar-Ripoll (2017). *"Neural Basis of Video Gaming: A Systematic Review"*. Frontiers in Human Neuroscience, 2017; 11 DOI:

10.3389/fnhum.2017.00248

18. Anna T. Prescott, James D. Sargent, Jay G. Hull. (2018). *"Metaanalysis of the relationship between violent video game play and physical aggression over time"*. Proceedings of the National Academy of Sciences, 2018; 115 (40): 9882 DOI: 10.1073/pnas.1611617114

19. Marzano, R. J. (2010). *"Using Games to Enhance Student Achievement. Meeting Students Where They Are"*, Educational Leadership, 67, 5, 71-72.

20. MacKenty, B. (2006). *"All Play and No Work"*. School Library Journal, 52, 46-48.

21. Ke, F., & Grabowski, B. (2007). *"Gameplay for maths learning: cooperative or not?"* British Journal of Educational Technology, 37, 249-259.

22. Esteban Pittaro (2018), *"How to help your kids avoid video game addition"*, https://www.aleteia.org/2018/10/17/how-to-help-your-kids-avoid-video-game-addition/amp/, accessed december, 2018

23. Kinman, T. (2017). *"What's the Difference between ADHD and ADD?"* https://www.healthline.com/health/adhd/difference-between-add-and-adhd, accessed December, 2018

24. Kulman, R. *"Video Games Can Help Kids with ADHD – If You Choose Wisely"*. https://www.additudemag.com/video-games-help-adhd/ accessed December, 2018

25. Gentile, D., Swing, E., Bowen, L., Ferlazzo, M. (2012). *"Video game playing can compound kids' existing attention problems says ISU study"*. https://archive.news.iastate.edu/news/2012/feb/VGattention, accessed October, 2018

26. Caroline Miller, *"Do Video Games Cause ADHD?"*, https://childmind.org/article/do-video-games-cause-adhd/, accessed November 2018

27. Molnar, M., Cavanagh, S. (2013). *"Consumer Demand for Digital Learning Games, Simulations Growing Worldwide"*.

https://www.edweek.org/ew/articles/2013/09/18/04games.h33.html

28. Barab, S. A.; Scott, B.; Siyahhan, S.; Goldstone, R.; Ingram-Goble, A.; Zuiker, S. J.; Warren, S. (2009). "*Transformational Play as a Curricular Scaffold: Using Videogames to Support Science Education*". Journal of Science Education and Technology. 18 (4): 305–320. doi:10.1007/s10956-009-9171-5.

29. Institute of Medicine, (2013), " *Educating the student body: taking physical activity and physical education to school*", Washington DC, National Academy of Science

30. Jesper Fritz (2017), "*Physical Activity During Growth. Effects on Bone, Muscle, Fracture Risk and Academic Performance*", Lund University, Faculty of Medicine

31. Linda Gabriel (2010), "*Spark, The Revolutionary New Science of Exercise and the Brain*" by John J. Ratey, MD – Book Review,http://thoughtmedicine.com/2010/05/spark-the-revolutionary-new-science-of-exercise-and-the-brain-by-john-j-ratey-md-book-review/, accessed August 2018

32. Sheryl Gay Stolberg (2010), "Childhood Obesity Battle Is Taken Up by First Lady", http://www.nytimes.com/2010/02/10/health/nutrition/10obesity.html?module=inline accessed August 2018

33. Lauren Cassani Davis, (2015), " *When Mindfulness Meets the Classroom*", https://www.theatlantic.com/education/archive/2015/08/mindfulness-education-schools-meditation/402469/ accessed September 2018

34. Marlynn Wei, MD, JD (2016), "*More than just a game: Yoga for school-age children*", http://www.health.harvard.edu/blog/more-than-just-a-game-yoga-for-school-age-children-201601299055, accessed September 2018

35. "*Data and Statistics About ADHD*", 2003-3016, http://www.cdc.gov/ncbddd/adhd/data.html accessed September 2018

36. Grace Hwang Lynch (2015), *"The Importance of Art in Child Development"*, http://www.pbs.org/parents/education/music-arts/the-importance-of-art-in-child-development/ accessed September 2018

37. Krichevets, A.N., Sirotkina, E.B., Yevsevicheva, I.V. & Zeldin, L.M. (1994). *"Computer games as a means of movement rehabilitation"*. Disability and Rehabilitation: An International Multidisciplinary Journal, 17, 100-105,https://doi.org/10.1016/j.compedu.2009.04.001

38. Trevor G. Marshall and Trudy J. Rumann Heil (2016). *"Electrosmog and autoimmune disease"*. doi: 10.1007/s12026-016-8825-7.

39. Statista (2017), *"Distribution of video gamers worldwide in 2017"*, by age group and gender, https://www.statista.com/statistics/722259/world-gamers-by-age-and-gender/, accessed October 2018

40. Kapp, Karl (2012). *"The gamification of learning and instruction: Game-based methods and strategies for training and education"*. San Fransciso: Pfeiffer. ISBN 9781118096345.

41. Werbach, Kevin; Hunter, Dan (2012). *"For the Win: How Game Thinking Can Revolutionize Your Business"*. Philadelphia, PA: Wharton Digital Press. ISBN 978-1613630235.

42. Suzanne Holloway (2018), *"Gamification in Education: 4 Ways To Bring Games To Your Classroom"*, https://tophat.com/blog/gamification-education-class/, accessed November 2018

43. Lou Carlozo (2012), *"Why college students stop short of a degree"*, http://www.reuters.com/article/2012/03/27/us-attn-andrea-education-dropouts-idUSBRE82Q0Y120120327, accessed November 2018

44. Asha Pandey (2015), *"6 Killer Examples Of Gamification In eLearning"*, https://elearningindustry.com/6-killer-examples-gamification-in-elearning, accessed January 2019

45. Pavlus, John (2010). "*The Game of Life*". Scientific American. 303: 43–44. doi:10.1038/scientificamerican1210-43.

46. Lee, J.; Hammer, J. (2011). *"Gamification in education: What, how, why bother?"* (PDF). *Academic Exchange Quarterly*. **15** (2). Archived

from the original (PDF) on 2011-05-16.

47. "Entertainment Trends in America" report reveals that video games account for one-third of the average monthly core entertainment spending in the U.S., PORT WASHINGTON, NEW YORK, May 20, 2009https://www.npd.com/wps/portal/npd/us/news/press-releases/pr_090520/, accessed May, 2018

48. WHO/IARC press release 208, 31. Mai 2011)

www.ingramcontent.com/pod-product-compliance
Lightning Source LLC
LaVergne TN
LVHW091427190726
843491LV00006B/1642

* 9 7 8 3 9 8 2 0 7 7 8 4 0 *